Praise Page

"Social media have changed how we can influence each other, as well as how easily we can be influenced (no one wants to hear that, I know!). This volume examines many of the benefits and potential problems that are continuing to result. We can't manage something well without first understanding it."

**—Douglas A. Gentile, PhD, Distinguished Professor,
Psychology, Iowa State University**

"Don't let the fervor over blockchain technology, cryptocurrency, and NFTs mislead – the social media of Web 2.0 are here to stay. Fortunately, this third *Masters of Media* volume tackles the issues of social media with thoughtful depth and insightful creativity. I highly recommend it. "

**—Paul Wright, PhD, Professor and Director of
Communication Science, The Media School,
Indiana University Bloomington**

"There's no arguing that social media is the most powerful influencer on today's youth. In his latest manuscript, Masters of Media, Dr. Victor Strasburger lays it all out—the good, the bad, and the disturbing influence of social media on the world, families and kids. A must read for all parents to become wiser, more informed media consumers and learn to see through the conspiracies and misinformation to help protect your children."

**—Tanya Altmann, MD, FAAP,Pediatrician, Founder of
Calabasas Pediatrics Wellness Center**

i

"Drs. Strasburger, Hogan and their co-authors adeptly address the ever-evolving media and the tremendous impact it continues to exert on lives of youth. I found the chapters on social media and disinformation most gripping as these are areas where not just culture wars have been waged, but elections have been influenced. This insightful book provides a wonderful foundation upon which readers can become more savvy consumers and analysts of media and society. "

—Nusheen Ameenuddin, MD, MPH, MPA; Chair AAP
Council on Communications and Media

Friend or Foe

Friend or Foe

Tackling the Issue of Social Media in Schools

Edited by
Victor C. Strasburger and Marjorie Hogan

ROWMAN & LITTLEFIELD
Lanham • Boulder • New York • London

Published by Rowman & Littlefield
An imprint of The Rowman & Littlefield Publishing Group, Inc.
4501 Forbes Boulevard, Suite 200, Lanham, Maryland 20706
www.rowman.com

86-90 Paul Street, London EC2A 4NE

British Library Cataloguing in Publication Information Available

Library of Congress Cataloging-in-Publication Data

Names: Strasburger, Victor C., 1949- editor. | Hogan, Marjorie J., editor.
Title: Friend or foe : tackling the issue of social media in schools /
    edited by Victor C. Strasburger and Marjorie Hogan.
Description: Lanham, Maryland : Rowman & Littlefield, 2023. |
    Includes bibliographical references.
Identifiers: LCCN 2022039782 (print) | LCCN 2022039783 (ebook) |
    ISBN 9781475855159 (cloth) | ISBN 9781475855166 (paperback) |
    ISBN 9781475855173 (ebook)
Subjects: LCSH: Social media in education. | Media literacy.
Classification: LCC LB1044.87 .F76 2023 (print) | LCC LB1044.87 (ebook) |
    DDC 306.43—dc23/eng/20221007
LC record available at https://lccn.loc.gov/2022039782
LC ebook record available at https://lccn.loc.gov/2022039783

∞™ The paper used in this publication meets the minimum requirements of American
National Standard for Information Sciences—Permanence of Paper for Printed Library
Materials, ANSI/NISO Z39.48-1992.

VCS: To Max and Katya, my two very media-literate children, and to Alya, who grew up without a TV.

MH: To Dave, always my support and model for healthy media habits.

Contents

Introduction

Victor C. Strasburger, MD and Marjorie Hogan, MD

All is flux. Nothing stays still.
—Ancient Greek philosopher Heraclitus.

Things change.
—American playwright David Mamet

I doubt I would be here [in the White House] if it weren't for social media, to be honest with you. . . . When somebody says something about me, I am able to go *bing, bing, bing* and I take care of it.
—President Donald Trump, quoted
by Reuters, October 22, 2017

Times are changing, and with them media are changing as well. Sometimes we forget that smartphones didn't come into common usage until well after the iPhone was first introduced in 2007. Facebook started up in 2004, and iPads in 2010. In another decade or more, people will probably communicate via holograms (and travel via flying cars).

Critics are quick to point out that with every new medium seems to come shock and awe, followed by anxiety and panic. First dime store novels, then comic books, followed by video games, and now social media. There was even anxiety when telephones were first introduced, with some people worrying that men and women would make secret plans. Are anxiety and panic justified? No. But people can be rightfully concerned about the potential plusses and minuses of any new medium.

In this slim volume, we attempt to elucidate some of the positives and negatives of social media. Clearly, the research is evolving, and with more longitudinal studies will come far more answers about behavioral effects of social media, both positive and negative. But we hope that this will serve as a beginning attempt in some small way, and we thank our coauthors vociferously.

Chapter 1

Social Media

Prosocial or Risky for Tweens and Teens?

Marjorie Hogan, MD

WHEN SOCIAL MEDIA ARE PROSOCIAL

Social media can be defined in myriad ways:

- Wikipedia: "social media are primarily internet-based tools for sharing and discussing information among human beings" (Wikipedia, 2022).
- Oxford Dictionary: "social media are websites and applications that enable users to create and share content or to participate in social networking" (Oxford Dictionary, 2022).

This chapter aims to explain general benefits offered by social networking, then will cover risks of social media use—both known and presumed—followed by recommendations to optimize and learn more about social media into the future. Chapter 2 is a discussion of social media relevance for more discrete groups of youth.

Young people love social media and by age group are avid users. A recent poll of parents of children and tweens found that approximately one-third of children aged seven to nine years and almost half of children aged ten to twelve years use social media apps (C.S. Mott Children's Hospital National Poll on Children's Health, 2021). Another survey found nearly 20 percent of tweens use social media daily. A whopping 84 percent of teens report using social media (and for nearly 90 minutes daily), but interestingly, only one-third enjoy social media a lot (Rideout et al., 2022). In its latest report on Media Use by Tweens and Teens, Common Sense Media found that media use in general grew faster between 2019 and 2021 than it did in the previous prepandemic four years. Other major findings included (Rideout et al., 2022):

1. Use of all screen media is up 17 percent since the start of the pandemic.
2. Children in higher-income homes have greater access to a computer than do children in middle- or lower-income homes.
3. Watching online videos is the favorite media activity for tween and teens.
4. Social media use is growing among tweens.
5. When forced to choose, more teens prefer YouTube over other platforms.
6. One form of media that did not increase during the pandemic was reading.

The era of Facebook (now Meta) seems to be ending. A 2017 survey found Instagram and Snapchat to be the most popular sites with teens and that 91 percent used the text message feature on mobile phones to connect with friends (Young, 2017). The highly regarded PEW survey (2018) found YouTube, Instagram, and Snapchat most popular with teens. "Fully 95% of teens have access to a smartphone, and 45% say they are online 'almost constantly'" (Anderson & Jiang, 2018). By 2021, preferences shifted, with 35 percent of teens surveyed choosing Snapchat as their favorite site, followed by 30 percent choosing TikTok and Instagram 22 percent. Only a mere 2 percent of teens spent time on Facebook or Twitter. At the same time, the teens surveyed spent approximately 4.2 hours per day on social media (Beer, 2021).

Common Sense Media's recent national survey found YouTube, TikTok, Snapchat, and Instagram to be the top four sites for online activity (Rideout et al., 2022). *And yet, it is important to point out that "watching television—whether through broadcast, cable, or streaming services—continues to be a mainstay of young people's media diets"* (Rideout et al., 2022). The 2021 National Survey of Social Media use from Edison Research and Triton Digital found that social media use has continued its annual increase among all age groups, but that TikTok is particularly popular among young people. Again, Facebook declined in popularity in this same group (Baer, 2021).

Adolescent developmental tasks provide necessary stepping stones and strengths as youth negotiate the sometimes difficult years between childhood and adulthood—not all arrive unscathed or at the same time. Despite the understandable angst about social media's impact on youth (more about that later), let us focus on the potential benefits: tweens (generally ten to twelve years old) and early adolescents form their identities through the reflection of family, friends, school, and connection with the community and wider world. The centrality of peers during these formative years, as youth disengage from parents, family, and other key adults, grounds them—for entertainment, affirmation, and identity. Social media serve as an adjunct, perhaps even as a "super-peer" in this process (Strasburger et al., 2014).

Benefits of social media in the lives of young people fall into a few categories. First, access to and presence on social media "can help kids do good" (Knorr, 2018). The literature and news are replete with examples of youth finding purpose and/or a voice through social networking. Famously, many of the teens surviving the Parkland massacre in Florida turned to social media to highlight the need for gun control via a national school walk-out (Kramer & Harlan, 2019). Students have also organized on social media to protest school budget cuts, and recently, the oppressive anti-transgender laws being passed in many states.

Common Sense Media published "Sites That Help Kids Do Good," encouraging positive education, social justice, and action for tweens and teens (e.g., Habitat for Humanity, It Gets Better) (Common Sense Media, 2018). In 2021, Smart Social highlighted eleven amazing teen-fueled projects, achieved through social media presence, ranging from gathering school supplies for disadvantaged students to educating about cyberbullying and real-life bullying to creating a nonprofit to benefit children of slain police officers to working to end world hunger (Smart Social, 2020).

Second, social media can strengthen friendships and enhance connection between peers and family. During the pandemic, social networking allowed isolated tweens and teens to maintain bonds with friends to some extent (although the effects of isolation and loneliness are only now being reported).

Third, tweens and teens seek to find and become comfortable with their identity. Exploration of "who am I" with online peers or groups may feel safer that face-to face contact for some. Affirmation of self and a sense of "belonging" are crucial tasks for teens in adolescence.

Next, for some youth, online connection may provide support and acceptance in difficult times. A young person with depression or suicidal notions could find immediate help. Information about health is also broadly available through validated sources on social networking sites.

Finally, social media sites offer an opportunity for youth to express themselves in myriad ways—and to get affirmation for their efforts. Producers of videos or photography, writers of fiction or poetry, educators about sports or hobbies, activists in any realm can reach a wide audience by uploading their craft onto social media.

A slightly older but expansive review of the role of social media in impacting youth well-being identified eight key domains, specifically: physical and mental health; identity and belonging; formal and informal learning; play and recreation; consumer practices; civic and political engagement; risk and safety; and, family and intergenerational relationships (Collin et al., 2015). Among other findings, the review identified that positive and negative impacts are contextual and that "children and young people bring to their social media use pre-existing social, cultural, political, emotional and psychological experiences and status." Although the effects are broadly positive, the harmful outcomes cannot be ignored. "It is the ways in which [youth] interact with social media to produce identity, community and culture that provide the clearest insight into the role of social media for wellbeing" (Collin et al., 2015).

A very large longitudinal study using two datasets analyzed estimates of social media use and life satisfaction ratings for different age groups. Findings suggest "distinct developmental windows of sensitivity to social media in adolescence, when higher estimated social media use predicts a decrease in life satisfaction ratings one year later" (Orben et al., 2022). The authors propose that the many developmental tasks during adolescence (cognitive development, emotional regulation, future planning, and complex sociocultural changes and transitions) may magnify the influence of peer perception—and heighten sensitivity to social media interactions and responses. Interestingly, older teens with either very low or very high social media use reported lower rating of life satisfaction compared to those with moderate use. Younger teens did not evidence this "Goldilocks hypothesis," rather a linear relationship with no decrease in life satisfaction at lower levels of social media use (Orben et al., 2022).

A 2021 systematic review of nineteen high-quality studies examined social media through the lens of adolescent users' perception of well-being. A thematic meta-synthesis found the four themes of "connections, identity, learning and emotions" related to teen well-being (Bronfenbrenner Center, 2021; Shankleman et al., 2021). As with many external influences in adolescent life, social media use may lead to both positive and negative outcomes.

- The first theme examined—connections—refers to a young person's relationships with others, friends, and family. Participants in the studies analyzed found that social networking can create intimacy with peers, enhance popularity, and allow more reticent youth an opportunity to make friends. Seven of the nineteen studies concluded that social media provided support and reassurance for young users. However, in the majority of the papers, youth gave examples of bullying, threats, or criticism during interactions, negative affecting connections with others. Youth reported that social media also harmed their connections with others (Bronfenbrenner Center, 2021; Shankleman et al., 2021).
- In terms of the second theme, identity, many participants described how social media helped them to "come out of their shells" and express their "true identities." The ability to share their thoughts and use chosen images improved self-expression and self-confidence. Conversely, in eight studies,

youth worried that representations could be "inauthentic" (Bronfenbrenner Center, 2021; Shankleman et al., 2021).

- Study youth felt that learning, the third theme studied, could be improved through exposure to new ideas, topics, and events, for example, the Black Lives Matter movement. Not surprisingly, in several studies, youth reported checking phones constantly, disrupting education, and also leading to inadequate sleep.
- Emotions, the fourth theme, also featured different responses from youth. In eleven of the nineteen studies, social media use led to positive emotions, including laughter, excitement, and boosting mood. Others felt that social networking offered stress management, alleviating anger or boredom. However, "in nearly all of the papers included in the review, participants said social media was a source of worry and pressure" (Bronfenbrenner Center, 2021; Shankleman et al., 2021), whether because of concern about judgment by others, embarrassment about images, concern about privacy or the indelible digital footprint, pressure to respond, or encountering disturbing content.

Social Media Use and the Pandemic

Use of social media increased during the pandemic (Rideout et al., 2022), not surprising given lockdowns, periods of quarantine, and prolonged schooling from home. Indeed, distance learning required children and teens to use technology to communicate with school and teachers, to compete assignments, and to "attend" classes. About 80 percent of youth ages eight to eighteen went online to learn. Even more impressive, social media became the connection—the glue—for many young people with friends and family. Loneliness and isolation are devastating conditions for many youth who need connection and affirmation. Common Sense Media produced a special report on the role of media during the pandemic (Rideout & Robb, 2021) listing several salient findings:

- A total of 84 percent used entertainment media during the pandemic to improve their mood.
- 81 percent to stay connected to friends and family.
- A total of 91 percent simply used media to have fun.
- 70 percent played video games to connect with friends.
- 56 percent used digital media to video chat.
- 40 percent watched media offerings with friends online.
- 78 percent used digital media to learn to do something new or to create.
- Black youth (compared to White peers) used more media to stay connected.
- Boys played more video games online, while girls tended to video chat.

Happily, the Common Sense Survey found that a pandemic bonus for youth was spending more time with family. Children and teens surveyed also reported being more excited than before the pandemic to get together in person with friends (Rideout & Robb, 2021).

A midpandemic study of nearly 600 college students with moderate or higher stress due to COVID-19 was randomly assigned to receive online self-help support or was referred to usual care. The online self-help group received cognitive-behavioral therapy and positive psychology principles to support resilience and coping. The online self-help group had greater improvement in symptoms of stress and depression at the end of the intervention; these outcomes persisted at follow-up (Rackoff et al., 2022).

A 2022 blog featured benefits of social media for tweens and teens (Raising Children, 2020):

- Digital media literacy; learning about safety, privacy, and exploration
- Collaborative learning; harnessing social media sites for education
- Creativity
- Fostering connectivity and communication with family and friends

In a recent discussion with teens about the benefits and risks of social media, one teen summarized their thoughts this way: "Social media connects each and every one of us in one way or another" (Hinduja, 2021).

RISKS OF SOCIAL MEDIA

A majority of U.S. parents (66 percent) believe that "parenting is harder today than it was 20 years ago," with many in this group citing technology as a reason why (Auxier et al., 2020). Children and teens are in front of screens for hours daily, whether traditional media (television) or digital media on mobile phones, iPads, and computers. The harmful effects of media, particularly "new media" get plenty of airtime. In many families, these media platforms are new to parents and grandparents, as opposed to their digital native offspring—and so create angst, fear, and blame. This chapter has detailed the known positive benefits of social media for teens and tweens, but no one denies the potential downsides and risks of the selfsame platforms and habits they engender.

Intuitively, some of the harmful effects of social media for young people are similar to well-researched negative impacts from traditional media, generally television and video games. Time spent with any screen leads to displacement from homework, face-to-face interaction with family and friends, active physical pursuits, hobbies, and simple daydreaming. In this respect, social networking online is no different from watching a television series. Online activity, whether passively absorbing or creating material, is sedentary and puts young social media users at risk for obesity and associated health risks. For decades, the existing research on media content, particularly violent and/or graphically sexual content, shows a relationship between the media images and messages and real-life attitudes and behavior—there is no reason to doubt social media images and messages convey the same risk.

Media in all forms is big business; advertising and commercial interests drive media content and lure eyes and ears to platforms. Young viewers are influenced by and susceptible to advertising. Research on social media impact is still emerging.

In the recent book *Death of Childhood*, Dr. Vic Strasburger explores the question of "why" media messages and images impact young viewers (Strasburger, 2020). These are salient not only for traditional media but also for new, transportable digital media, as well:

- Media give kids "scripts" for how to act in certain situations. Youth lack experience in so many situations and parents can't teach and model everything.
- Media provide compelling, accessible education as "a super sex educator, a super drug educator, a super educator about human behavior."
- Media also give youth attractive peer and adult role models to emulate. Celebrity influencers wield terrific power in the minds of adolescents.
- Media act as a "super-peer," basically normalizing attitudes and behaviors, giving young people misinformation and carte blanche for risky behavior (Strasburger et al., 2014).

A longtime documented harm from screen media use is sleep disturbance, and social media use likewise impacts sleep quality and quantity for youth. "Checking social media, sending emails, or looking at the news before bed can keep us awake, as nighttime use of electronics can affect sleep through the stimulating-effects of light from digital screens" (Newsom, 2022). Research finds that "the more time adolescents spent on screen-based activities (like social media, web surfing, watching TV, and gaming), the more trouble they had falling asleep and the less sleep they got during the night. These sleep issues were then linked with increased symptoms of insomnia and depression" (Li et al., 2019; Newsom, 2022).

A cross-sectional study of teens in Iran found that nearly a third of the adolescents sleep duration was 6 hours or less, and it was correlated with the amount of time smart devices were used; and poor quality sleep, fewer hours of sleep, and dysfunction during daytime hours were linked to social media use (Pirdehghan et al., 2021).

Sleep variables (insomnia and sleep duration) were found to fully mediate the association between social messaging, web-surfing, TV watching, and depressive symptoms in a 2019 study of nearly 2,900 teens. A 2021 systematic review found an association between high levels of social media use in youth with poor mental health outcomes as well as poor sleep quality. Some studies in this review showed sleep quality to mediate the relationship between social media use and poor mental health outcomes (Alonzoa et al., 2021).

Burgeoning research in the possible association between social media use and mental health disorders in youth has not revealed clear answers. Many researchers have observed the rise in adolescent mental health diagnoses over the past decade in conjunction with the merging popularity of social media platforms and networking (Keles et al., 2020; Richtel, 2022; Rideout & Fox, 2018; Stoilova et al., 2021; Twenge et al., 2022); however, there is still discussion about causality versus correlation of these findings. Rideout and colleagues conducted a national survey of social media habits for over 1,330 teens, also administering a validated survey to measure depressive symptoms. Many youth reported that social media "helps them find connection, support, and inspiration during times of depression, stress, or anxiety." Key findings included the following (Rideout & Fox, 2018):

- For youth with significant depression, 30 percent say social media is "very" important to them for feeling less alone (compared to 7 percent without) and 27 percent say it is "very" important for getting inspiration from others (compared to 13 percent).
- A total of 30 percent of youth with depression reported that when feeling depressed, stressed, or anxious, using social media makes them feel better as opposed to 22 percent feeling worse.
- Surveyed youth with significant depression reported often feeling left out on social media sites (18 percent versus 1 percent) or believing that other teens are feeling better (32 percent versus 7 percent).

Optimistically, study youth reporting moderate-to-severe symptoms of depression do turn to the Internet for support and information, "including researching mental health issues online (90%), accessing other people's health stories through blogs, podcasts, and videos (75%), using mobile apps related to well-being (38%), and connecting with health providers through digital tools such as texting and video chat (32%)" (8). Young females are more likely than male peers to seek information about anxiety (55 percent versus 29 percent) or depression (49 percent versus 27 percent) (Rideout & Fox, 2018).

A recent systematic review of relevant studies looked at four social media variables: time spent, activity level, investment, and addictive behavior. For eligibility, the studies involved teen participants, measurement of social media use, and validated measures of mental health outcomes (Keles et al., 2020). After analysis, "prominent risk factors for depression, anxiety and psychological distress emerging . . . comprised time spent on social media, activities such as repeated checking for messages, personal investment, and addictive or problematic use." However, the authors stressed that findings were mixed, and by no means conclusive, perhaps complicated by family support and sleep-related factors (Keles et al., 2020).

A 2021 multimethod pilot study from the United Kingdom focused on Internet/social media use and its relationship to teen mental health, specifically in those teens with preexisting mental health problems. Although the literature review confirmed that excessive Internet use is a risk factor for mental health problems, there were several more nuanced findings including (Stoilova et al., 2021):

- Youth with eating disorders or a history of self-harm were more likely to seek related online content.
- Being exposed to related online content "can trigger or encourage problematic behaviour" according to a review of relevant studies.
- "Online communities dedicated to eating disorders or self-harm, and participation in such communities can be both supportive and harmful for adolescents."
- Online forums may offer immediate help to youth in distress "who feel they have nowhere else to turn."
- Online communities seem to offer youth with mental health concerns "a sense of validation and belonging."
- The risk of self-harm or eating disorders more likely results in excessive digital engagement rather than the converse.

In the same multimethod study, focus groups with both teen and expert participants found the following (Stoilovga et al., 2021):

- Youth participants identified that social media offered both benefits and risks, offering not only connectivity and support but also risk of exacerbating extant mental health symptoms.
- Those youth with ADHD reported "losing the sense of time" while online and the real risk of posting impulsively.
- Youth with a history of self-harm noted the Internet is a ready source of new ways to inflict harm or trigger self-harm.

- Participants with a history of disordered eating discussed the aesthetic aspects of digital social media content, which can lead to making unhelpful comparisons with others.

In general, the focus groups concluded that poor mental health is associated with exposure to other online risks for youth with self-harm or eating disorder histories, such as cyberbullying, misinformation, or harassment. For parents and other adults, realizing that a teen is experiencing mental health problems is tricky—online activity can be very private and youth may choose to spare families and friends from their struggles with mental health or to prevent embarrassment. Online communities can offer a valuable resource for teens struggling with mental health.

Twenge et al. (2022) posed a question: "Why did rates of depression, anxiety, loneliness, dissatisfaction with life, self-harm, suicide attempts, and suicides begin rising among adolescents around 2012" (Twenge et al., 2022)? Using data from the Millennium Cohort Study (UK), which studies nearly 20,000 children, the team employed a novel technique (specification curve analysis) to examine the relationship between social media use and several measures of mental health (as opposed to previous studies that used all forms of media). Logic demands consideration of other factors beyond social media to explain whether there is a link to rising social media use, but they found *a consistent and substantial association between mental health and social media use* (Twenge et al., 2022). The analysis found that social media use (not just generic screen time) for girls (not all youth) showed a much larger relationship with poor mental health. For comparison purposes, this relationship was comparable to other factors, such as "binge drinking, sexual assault, obesity, and drug use including heroin use" (Twenge et al., 2022).

Twenge summarized her previous and current research in a 2022 blog, noting the following (Bard, 2022):

- For youth using social media more than five hours daily, depression is twice as likely than for nonusers (higher depression rates tend to begin after one hour online).
- General screen media use (TV, gaming, texting) is less strongly associated with depression (higher depression rates occur after three to four hours of daily use).

A 2021 study using data from the Monitoring the Future Study concluded that "contrary to the popular narrative, daily social media use is not a strong or consistent risk factor for depressive symptoms" (Kreski et al., 2021) in youth without preexisting mental health vulnerability.

A revelatory 2020 study by Odgers and Jensen acknowledges the increase in social media use in adolescence, and that "epidemiological data suggest that adolescents may spend more hours each day communicating with peers via electronically mediated platforms than they do sleeping, attending school, or interacting with adults" (Odgers & Jensen, 2020; Prinstein et al., 2020). However, this annual research review challenges the "purported link between digital media use and adolescent psychopathology" and demonstrated that the specific number of hours teens spend on social media is not reliably associated with depression, anxiety, and risk behaviors. The authors claim that extant research has used "a paucity of longitudinal data," insufficient reliance on theoretical frameworks, and has not incorporated the influence of a rapidly changing media landscape (Odgers & Jensen, 2020; Prinstein et al., 2020).

The authors used several methodologies to conclude that there is little evidence of connections between social media use and mental health symptoms. In fact, "adolescents who report more connectivity via text messaging and communication tend to report fewer mental health symptoms of depression and anxiety" (Odgers & Jensen, 2020; Prinstein et al., 2020). The authors decry the persistent negative association made between social media and teen mental health and the lack of careful scientific study (Odgers, 2021). They emphasize that lower family socioeconomic status may contribute substantially to a teen's vulnerability on social media, possibly from receiving less guidance and support about being online. Stresses in real life and online may coexist and amplify, shaping both mental health and social media experiences (Odgers, 2021).

A large study from the United Kingdom in 2022 followed over 84,000 people (and over 17,400 adolescents) longitudinally to ascertain the relationship between social media use and life satisfaction. The researchers generally found a fairly weak relationship, but for youth (age ten to twenty-one years) they identified distinct periods of adolescence when heavy social media use and lower life satisfaction coincided: ages eleven to thirteen for girls and fourteen to fifteen for boys (pubertal years), but again at about age nineteen years for both sexes (Orben et al., 2022). Possibly the sensitivity to social media use is related to transitions common in older adolescence.

A 2020 systematic review and meta-analysis evaluated the relationship between teen social media use and risky behaviors. It found "small-to-medium concurrent associations between higher levels of social media use and more frequent engagement in risky behaviors, including substance use and risky sexual behaviors" (Vannucci et al., 2020) certainly contributing to, but not solving the ongoing debate about social media's role in adolescent well-being.

Continuing the theme of risk behavior in adolescence, a 2022 study examined media new reports of twenty-five school shootings in the United States involving teenage males (Dowdell et al., 2022). The authors reported:

- The majority (88 percent) of school shooters had at least one social media account—75 percent had "posted disturbing content of guns and threatening messages."
- An adverse childhood event (ACE) was evident for nearly three-fourth of the shooters.
- A total of 60 percent reported being bullied in-person or on social media.

Although a definitive profile of a school shooter does not exist, youth at-risk can be screened for a history of being bullied and use of social media.

An extensive 2022 review of social media use and teen eating disorders amplifies the major concern of parents and clinicians. The association of traditional media and disorder eating and body image distortion is well known (Hogan & Strasburger, 2008), "but the proliferation of social media and rapid increase in the use of the Internet by adolescents generates new dynamics and new risks for the development and maintenance of eating disorders (Saul et al., 2022)." This review found the strongest relationship for those youth with high levels of engagement with social media, primarily with photo-based activities and platforms, such as Instagram and TikTok. These platforms are rife with portrayals of unrealistic and unrepresentative bodies and are "accompanied by a discourse that exaggerates the extent to which body weight and shape are controllable through diet and exercise" (Saul et al., 2022). Teens spending more time investing in their selfies—editing, possibly not posting—tended to self-report a higher likelihood of eating disorder symptoms. As well, a mixed-gender group of adolescents posting images, but either not receiving any feedback (no likes) or receiving negative feedback, reported increased symptoms.

A very recent cross-sectional study from Korea, involving over 53,000 teens, researched the teens' smart phone use (duration and content) and any association with body image distortion and/or weight-loss behaviors (Kwon et al., 2020). The authors found body image distortion to be highly correlated with use of smart phones for entertainment-focused content in both males and females and that even moderate use of smartphones can lead to unhealthy consequences for body image. Idealized body images for both males and females are prevalent on digital platforms providing youth with images of the "ideal" body shape and appearance to internalize.

SOCIAL MEDIA REVELATIONS

The *Wall Street Journal* investigative team exploded a bombshell in 2021 into Facebook's sotto voce awareness of the harm the giant platform has wreaked on adolescents. The WSJ published many articles and documents, thanks in large part to a former Facebook employee whistleblower (Morrow, 2021). From the WSJ: "Time and again, the documents show Facebook's researchers have identified the platform's ill effects. Time and again, despite congressional hearings, its own pledges and numerous media exposés, the company didn't fix them. The trove of documents offers perhaps the clearest picture thus far of how broadly Facebook's problems are known inside the company, up to the chief executive himself" (Horwitz, 2021). Repeatedly, Facebook had documented the harm Instagram caused for users, most notably teenage girls, "a valuable but untapped audience" according to one 2020 document (Horwitz, 2021).

Internal research also found that Facebook use led to worse body image issues for one in three adolescent girls and that "teens blame Instagram for increases in the rate of anxiety and depression. . . . This reaction was unprompted and consistent across all groups" (Morrow, 2021). According to another leaked document from the whistleblower, two internal Facebook studies reported that 13.5 percent of British teen girls reported that Instagram increased suicidal thoughts and that for 17 percent of teen users, eating disorders worsened after Instagram use (Romo, 2021).

A second explosive *Wall Street Journal* investigative project in late 2021 found that TikTok, the popular video-sharing app, had created a dozen automated accounts registered as thirteen-year-olds and then the app's algorithm beamed tens of thousands of weight-loss videos within a few weeks of their joining the platform. When they go down rabbit holes of dangerous images and messages, vulnerable youth can absorb "potentially dangerous content such as emaciated images, purging techniques, hazardous diets, and body shaming" (Hobbs et al., 2021). Other such videos feature "the corpse bride diet" or quick weight-loss competitions—terribly hazardous and compelling fare for many young social media users. TikTok does not allow such content officially and has imposed some further restrictions since facing criticism; however, some hashtags have avoided the scrutiny (Paul, 2021).

A recent article in the *Washington Post* reported the sordid story of a twelve-year-old girl being befriended on Snapchat (the photo- and video-sharing app) by an adult male, ultimately being coerced into sending him nude photos. She believed the photos would disappear (a Snapchat feature), but he distributed her photos far and wide. The girl, now sixteen, and her mother are leading a class action lawsuit against the giant company (with 100s of millions of users), arguing issues of privacy, safety, and inadequate policies to protect children. The $50 billion company reported 90 percent of youth aged thirteen to twenty-four years use the platform—"a group it designated the 'Snapchat Generation'" (Harwell, 2022).

An unusual phenomenon has emerged over the course of the pandemic, noted in the not only in the United States but also in Canada, Europe, and

Asia, specifically a growing number of rapid onset functional tic disorders especially in adolescent girls. Patients were presenting to clinics with abnormal body and facial movements and vocalizations, but quite distinct from Tourette syndrome, a well-defined disorder mainly diagnosed in younger boys. These new tic disorders are "functional neurological disorders, a class of afflictions that includes certain vocal tics and abnormal body movements that aren't tied to an underlying disease" (Jargon, 2022). Although a causal relationship between stress due to COVID-19 and functional tic-like behaviors is not established, researchers surmise stress and uncertainty may play a role. As well, clinicians discovered that many of the teens had been watching TikTok videos of people who said they had Tourette syndrome, with the characteristic repetitive, involuntary movements and/or sounds before developing functional tics themselves.

The researchers hypothesize neuropsychiatric vulnerability and social media contagion as an explanation (Han et al., 2022). Many of the youth presenting with functional tic disorders reported preexisting stressors or a history of or concurrent mental health symptoms (such as suicidal ideation or anxiety) (Han et al., 2022; Pringsheim et al., 2021).

IDENTIFYING THE BENEFITS, REDUCING THE HARM OF SOCIAL MEDIA

Media will not stop evolving. Every iteration, every innovation engenders excitement, angst, and acceptance (maybe), then the cycle starts again. Social media—digital, transportable, accessible—a template for innovation, for aspiration, for our better angels and our most vile impulses . . . here we are in 2022. Are the kids OK?

Research and perspective teach us that social media are life-changing for some youth, but a dangerous siren for others. How do we balance social media's possibilities with its potential harm? Hopefully, this chapter has made clear that developmentally, social media have much to offer to teens seeking identity, affirmation, support, and possibility—the real tasks of adolescence. At the same time, youth are vulnerable, and social media messages and images can elevate or discourage, or even cyberbully. Social media offer glimpses of and experiences with peers around the world—with sympathetic needs and goals. They offer community to some youth who are experiencing barriers and lack of support and affirmation in the real world.

Responsibility to harness the great potential of social media rests with parents, teachers, health care professionals, sociologists, and certainly, youth voices are essential. At the same time, the danger posed by social media's power and reach is indisputable.

More research on social media and the impact of children and youth is urgently needed. By the time a platform is highlighted as problematic, research is initiated, and funding is procured, the media scene has evolved (Strasburger, 2020). The popular social media platforms of the day change—witness the ascendance of Instagram, TikTok, and YouTube for teens and the decline of Facebook. Where should research energy and dollars be focused?

Having adolescent presence in monitoring, researching, and creating product on social media is essential. Teens can identify problems and risks on social media, and they know what they want and need. Experts are aware that more research about social media is needed, for example (Prinstein, 2020):

- How to benefit youth from underrepresented or at-risk backgrounds, including members of ethnic, racial, gender, and sexual minority groups?
- How to harness its power for the "development of rapid and nuanced communication skills, the solicitation and provision of empathy for even minor daily hassles, identity exploration, artistic creativity, and perhaps even increasingly gender-balanced opportunities to safely express emotional vulnerability" (Prinstein, 2020).
- How to guide questions regarding the putative developmental risks associated with digital media use?
- What are the specific behaviors that adolescents engage online, as well as individual differences in their motivations, rather than a focus on time spent online?
- What are the demographic or psychological characteristics are that create unique vulnerabilities?
- What is the intersection between teen brain development and digital media usage is; for example, reward and stimulation?
- What are the differences are between online and offline social constructs?

These authors thus set forth an ambitious research agenda to optimize the relationship between adolescents and social media sites, and they "hope that the message conveyed is that . . . digital media does . . . matter for adolescent mental health, [and] well-designed and interpreted studies on this topic are more important than ever. Digital media is here to stay" (Prinstein, 2020).

Researchers, physicians, and teachers clearly have a role in optimizing social media for youth; parents also can be a positive force to harness the benefits and limit the harm of social networking for tween and teens. The *New York Times* published a simple, realistic set of guidelines for parents to reduce screen time, relevant for both television and new digital media (Talib, 2020).

- "Start the conversation"; even over dinner or after a show or documentary, discuss as a family—age appropriately—discuss the benefits and pitfalls of media. This is media literacy at work.

- Take stock of parent media use. How much time do you spend on your phone?—Eliminate time, apps, platforms reasonably. "Parents modeling healthy relationships with their phones is the most influential part of family digital well-being" (Talib, 2020).
- Use your phone and do not let it use you; do not multitask.
- Create device-free zones and times (dinner and bedtime absolutely).
- Make a family plan for media, for example, the American Academy of Pediatrics' Family Media Use Plan (healthychildren.org/familymediaplan) (American Academy of Pediatrics, 2016)

The Stanford Center for Youth Mental Health and Wellbeing pursued an exploratory qualitative research project to understand both the negative and positive impact of social media on teens' wellbeing. This project elevated the opinions and needs of teens and the following were key findings of the project (Harrison, 2022):

- Youth participants encounter graphic content on social media, but do not see how to cope with it and generally do not seek support for any distress.
- Youth surveyed identified strategies to cope with negative experiences on social media.
- Youth use social media to make themselves feel good.
- Youth surveyed seek positive uses for social media, specifically options for creativity.
- Ads make teens feel a lack of control.
- Youth report at least some parent/family involvement with social media.

Recognizing these findings, the project identified several strategies to move forward, most self-evident (Harrison, 2022):

- Identify opportunities for families to engage with youth using social media, for connection and guidance;
- Limit exposure to graphic portrayals and further explore the implications of youth exposure to violence or other graphic material;
- Establish ways to limit teens' exposure to advertising on social media;
- Discuss and develop strategies for teens to identify, approach, and confront hateful or bullying behavior on social media;
- Develop social media literacy;
- Set appropriate goals for social media use: creativity, connection;
- Explore how different emotional states change interpretation and experiences online.

Thus, social media impact four distinct areas for youth: connections, identity, learning, and emotions (Bronfenbrenner Center, 2021). A recent systematic review found that in all four domains, positive and negative outcomes were reported by youth.

Parents are struggling with balancing children's use of screens and digital media. Most say that parenting is more challenging today than ever in the past (Auxier et al., 2020). The Lurie Children's Hospital in Chicago surveyed nearly 3000 parents, finding their greatest concerns to be related to media: children not getting enough sleep, children being less physically active, and, children not focusing on homework (Lurie Children's Blog, 2020). Parents also noted the increase in time spent on social media by teens and expressed concern about specific platforms—Instagram and Snapchat. A majority of parents surveyed expressed their belief that social media threaten social and psychological health, specifically that teens are not socializing normally, they have an unhealthy desire for attention and approval online, and that teens may be addicted to their phones (Lurie Children's Blog, 2020).

Privacy and online safety are additional worries for parents of tweens and teens. Resources for parents, families, and other stakeholder adults exist and can provide direction for optimizing social networking for youth. The figure below illustrates powerfully how high concern about social media use—for Black, White and Latino parents—ranks among a recent poll (2020) of Top Child Health Concerns (C.S. Mott Children's Hospital National Poll on Children's Health, 2021).

The Digital Wellness Lab at Harvard/Boston Children's Hospital aims to help parents navigate the digital age with their children. The Lab studies teens' use and the positive and negative effects of their digital media use. A myriad of topics are addressed for parents: cell phone use, video gaming, fear of missing out (FOMO) on social media, cyberbullying, and many more. The Lab can be accessed at digitalwellnesslab.org (figure 1.1) (Digital Wellness Lab, 2022).

Raising Children Network from Australia, an accessible and useful website about media for parents, offers a great deal of up-to-date information as well. The website features definitions of social media as well as discussion of both the known benefits and risks for children and teens. The material on managing social media risks is particularly helpful:

- Talking honestly and openly about social media use and habits;
- Discussing how youth should treat other people and be treated online;
- Understanding the risks involved in using social media;
- Learning how to navigate the risks;
- Learning what to do if people ask for personal details, are mean or abusive online, post embarrassing photos, or share information.

A great deal more substantive information is available, including learning more about social media and platforms; thinking about children's ages and social media recommendations; banning of social media; use guidelines (re:

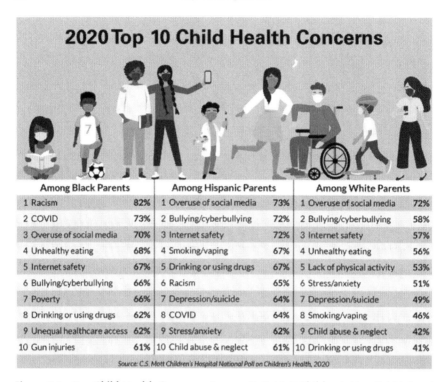

Figure 1.1   Top Child Health Concerns. *Source*: C. S. Mott Children's Hospital National Poll on Children's Health, 2021.

homework); time permitted; media-free zones; privacy; appropriateness of postings and images; and safety. The website can be accessed at raisingchildren.net.au (Raising Children, 2020).

Internet Matters, another parent-friendly website devoted to expert support and practical tips to help children benefit from technology in a safe and smart manner. Parents can access strategies and support for online safety, optimizing education, privacy, and multiple other technology-related topics. This resource can be accessed at internetmatters.org (Internet Matters, 2022).

Common Sense Media is a perennial favorite and outstanding resource for beneficial, educational, and fun media for youth. It rates and gives information about a wide variety of media, including movies, TV, books, games, and apps and can be accessed at commonsensemedia.org (Common Sense Media, 2022).

The University of Minnesota Extension Service website has published a PDF on "Teens and Social Media Use," also offering an easy to understand, useful review of the benefits and risks of social media use as well as tips for parents to optimize digital media habits in the home, including stressing safety and online behavior. The University of MN website for parents can be accessed at extension.umn.edu/tough-topics-kids (University of MN Extension Service, 2022).

Without question, social media use in tweens and teens leads to both positive and negative effects and the outcome depends on many factors and variables. The challenge of new technologies is to understand and optimize the opportunities and identify and mitigate the harm.

Using social media for identity, connection, and entertainment may enhance the challenging adolescent years for many youth. Groups of teens experiencing marginalization or with special health needs definitely can glean support, information, and connection on social media. "All screen time is not equal. We encourage parents to think less about the blunt measurement of screen time, and more carefully about how their children spend time on devices and what that means for their social development. . . . Adolescents' online risk often reflects offline vulnerabilities, which means it is likely that many of the strategies that guide how we promote healthy development and effective parenting will apply when supporting youth in online activities and experiences" (Lurie Children's Blog, 2020).

REFERENCES FOR PART 1

Alonzoa, R., Hussain, J., Stranges, S., & Anderson, K. K. (2021). Interplay between social media use, sleep quality, and mental health in youth: A systematic review. *Sleep Medicine Reviews*, *56*, 101414. https://doi.org/10.1016/j.smrv.2020.101414

American Academy of Pediatrics. (2016). *Family media plan.* Elk Grove Village, IL. https://healthychildren.org

Anderson, M. A., & Jiang, J. (2018). *Teens, social media and technology.* Washington, D.C.: Pew Research Center. https://www.pewresearch.org

Auxier, B., Anderson, M., Perrin, A., & Turner, E. (2020). *Parenting children in the age of screens.* Washington, D.C.: Pew Research Center. https://www.pewresearch.org

Baer, J. (2021). *Social media usage statistics for 2021 reveal surprising shifts.* Phoenix, AZ: Convince & Convert. https://www.convinceandconvert.com

Bard, S. C. (2022). *Social media and kids' mental health: Q&A with Jean Twenge.* San Diego, CA: South Diego State University. https://newscenter.sdsu.edu

Beer, T. (2021, October 14). *More than 1 in 3 teens say Snapchat is their favorite social media app, only 2* percent *cite Facebook, survey finds.* Jersey City, NJ: Forbes. https://www.forbes.com

Bronfenbrenner Center. (2021). The pros and cons of social media for youth. *Psychology Today*, New York, NY. https://www.psychologytoday.com

Collin, P., Swist, T., McCormack, J., & Third, A. (2015). *Social media and the well-being of children and young people: A literature review.* Institute for Culture and Society, University of Western Sydney for the Commissioner for Children and Young People, Western Australia. https://apo.org.au

Common Sense Media. (2018). *Sites that help kids do good.* San Francisco, CA: Common Sense. https://www.commonsensemedia.org

Common Sense Media. (2022). San Francisco, CA: Common Sense. https://www.commonsensemedia.org

C.S. Mott Children's Hospital National Poll on Children's Health. (2021, October). *National poll: 1/3 of children ages 7-9 use social media apps.* Ann Arbor, MI: University of Michigan. www.mottpoll.org

Digital Wellness Lab. (2022). Boston, MA: Boston Children's Hospital. https://www.digitalwellnesslab.org

Dowdell, E. B., Frwitas, E., Owens, A., & Greenle, M. M. (2022). School shooters: Patterns of adverse childhood experiences, bullying, and social media. *Journal of Pediatric Health Care, 36,* 339–346. https://doi.org/10.1016/j.pedhc.2021.12.004

Han, V. X., Kozlowska, K., Lorentzos, M., Wong, W. K., Mohammed, S. S., Savage, B., Chudleigh, C., & Dale, R. C. (2022). Rapid onset functional tic-like behaviours in children and adolescents during COVID-19: Clinical features, assessment and biopsychosocial treatment approach. *Journal of Pediatric Child Health.* Advance online publication. https://doi10.1111/jpc.15932

Harrison, V. (2022). *Social media and youth: Findings and recommendations from an investigation into teen experiences.* Palo Alto, CA: Stanford Medical School Department of Psychiatry and Behavioral Sciences. https://www.med.stanford.edu

Harwell, D. (2022). *A teen girl sexually exploited on Snapchat takes on American tech.* Washington, D.C.: The Washington Post. https://www.washingtonpost.com

Hinduja, S. (2021). *A teen's view of social media in 2021.* Cyberbullying Research Center. https://cyberbullying.org

Hobbs, T., Barry, Rob, & Koh, Y. (2021). *'The corpse bride diet': How TikTok inundates teens with eating-disorder videos.* New York, NY: The Wall Street Journal. https://www.wsj.com

Hogan, M. J., & Strasburger, V. C. (2008). Body image, eating disorders, and the media. *Adolescent Medicine, 19,* 521–546.

Horwitz, J. (2021). *The Facebook files. A wall street journal investigation.* New York, NY: The Wall Street Journal. https://www.wsj.com

Internet Matters. (2022). London, U.K. https://www.internetmatters.org

Jargon, J. (2022). *Teen girls are still getting TikTok-related tics—And other disorders.* Washington, D.C.: The Washington Post. https://washington post.com

Keles, B., McCrae, N., & Grealish, A. (2020) A systematic review: The influence of social media on depression, anxiety and psychological distress in adolescents. *International Journal of Adolescence and Youth, 25,* 79–93. https://doi:10.1080/0 2673843.2019.1590851

Knorr, C. (2018, March 19). *Five ways social media can be good for teens.* Washington, D.C.: Washington Post. https://washingtonpost.com

Kramer, M., & Harlan, J. (2019, February 13). *Parkland shooting: Where gun control and school safety stand today.* New York, NY: New York Times. https://www.newyorktimes.com

Kreski, N., Platt, J., Rutherford, C., Olson, M., Odgers, C., Schulenberg, J., & Keyes, K. M. (2021). Social media use and depressive symptoms among United States adolescents. *Journal of Adolescents Health, 68*, 572–579. https://doi.org/10.1016/j.jadohealth.2020.07.006

Li, X., Buxton, O. M., Lee, S., Chang, A. M., Berger, L. M., & Hale, L. (2019). Sleep mediates the association between adolescent screen time and depressive symptoms. *Sleep Medicine, 57*, 51–60. https://doi: 10.1016/j.sleep.2019.01.029

Lurie Children's Blog. (2020). *Parenting teens in the age of social media.* Chicago, IL: Lurie Children's Hospital of Chicago. https://www.luriechildrens.org

Morrow, A. (2021). *Jaw-dropping moments in WSJ's bombshell Facebook investigation.* Atlanta, GA: CNN Business. https:www.cnn.org

Newsom, R. (2022). *Sleep and social media.* Sleep Foundation. https://www.sleep-foundation.org

Odgers, C. L., & Jensen, M. R. (2020). Annual research review: Adolescent mental health in the digital age: Facts, fears, and future directions. *Journal of Child Psychology and Psychiatry, 61*, 336–348. https://doi.org/10.1111/jcpp.13190

Odgers, C. L. (2021). Adolescent development and depression in the digital age: Frequently asked questions with fact- versus fear-based answers. In *Center for media, technology and democracy.* Montreal, Quebec, Canada: McGill University. https://www.mediatechdemocracy.com

Orben, A., Przybylski, A. K., Blakemore, S., & Kievit, R. A. (2022). Windows of developmental sensitivity to social media. *Nature Communications, 13*, 1649. https://www.nature.com/naturecommunications

Oxford Dictionary. (2022, March). *Social media.* Oxford Dictionary. https://www.oed.com

Paul, K. (2021). *'It spreads like a disease': How pro-eating-disorder videos reach teens on TikTok.* London, U.K.: The Guardian. https://www.theguaradian.com

Pirdehghan, A., Khezmeh, E., & Panahi, S. (2021). Social media use and sleep disturbance among adolescents: A cross-sectional study. *Iran Journal of Psychiatry, 16*, 137–145. https://doi:10.18502/ijps.v16i2.5814

Pringsheim, T., Ganos, C., McGuire, J. F., Hedderly, T., Woods, D., Gilbert, D. L., Piacentini, J., Dale, R. C., & Martino, D. (2021). Rapid onset functional tic like behaviors in young females during the COVID 19 pandemic. *Movement Disorder, 36*, 2707–2713. https://doi:10.1002/mds.28778

Prinstein, M. J., Nesi, J., & Telzer, E. H. (2020). Commentary: An updated agenda for the study of digital media use and adolescent development – Future directions following Odgers & Jensen. *Journal of Child Psychology and Psychiatry, 61*, 349–352. https://doi.org/10.1111/jcpp.13219

Rackoff, G. N., Fitzsommons-Craft, E. E., Taylor, C. B., Eisenberg, D., Wilfley, D. E., & Newman, M. G. (2022). A randomized controlled trial of internet-based self-help for stress during the COVID-19 pandemic. *Journal of Adolescent Health, 22*, e12775. https://doi.org/10.1016/j.jadohealth.2022.01.227

Raising Children. (2020). *Social media benefits and risks: Children and teenagers raising children.* http://www.raisingchildren.net.au

Richtel, M. (2022). *'It's life or death': The mental health crisis among U.S. teens.* New York, NY: New York Times. https://newyorktimes.com

Rideout, V., Fox, S., & Well Being Trust. (2018). Digital health practices, social media use, and mental well-being among teens and young adults in the U.S. *Articles, Abstracts, and Reports.* https://digitalcommons.psjhealth.org/publications/1093

Rideout, V., Peebles, A., Mann, S., & Robb, M. B. (2022). *Common sense census: Media use by tweens and teens, 2021.* San Francisco, CA: Common Sense. https://www.commonsensemedia.org

Rideout, V., & Robb, M. B. (2021). *The role of media during the pandemic: Connection, creativity, and learning for tweens and teens.* San Francisco, CA: Common Sense. https://www.commonsensemedia.org

Romo, V. (2021). *Whistleblower's testimony has resurfaced Facebook's Instagram problem.* Washington, D.C.: National Public Radio. https://www.npr.org

Saul, J., Rodgers, R. F., & Saul, M. (2022). Adolescent eating disorder risk and the social online world: An update. *Child and Adolescent Psychiatric Clinics of North America, 31*, 167–177. https://doi:01.1016/j.chc.2021.09.004

Shankleman, M., Hammond, L., & Jones, F. W. (2021). Adolescent social media use and well-being: A systematic review and thematic meta-synthesis. *Adolescent Research Review, 6*, 471–492. https://doi.org/10.1007/s40894-021-00154-5

Smart Social. (2020). *Eleven teens using social media for good deeds.* https://smart-social.com/post/teens-using-social-media-good-deeds

Stoilova, M., Edwards, C., Kostyrka-Allchorne, K., Livingstone, S., & Sonuga-Barke, E. (2021). *Adolescents' mental health vulnerabilities and the experience and impact of digital technologies: A multimethod pilot study.* London, UK: London School of Economics and Political Science and King's College London. https://doi.org/DOI: 10.18742/pub01-073

Strasburger, V. C. (2020). *The death of childhood: Reinventing the joy of growing up.* Cambridge, MA: Cambridge Scholars Press.

Strasburger, V. C., Wilson, B. J., & Jordan, A. B. (2014). *Children, adolescents and the media.* Thousand Oaks, CA: Sage Publishing.

Talib, H. (2020). *Five tips for reducing family screen time.* New York, NY. https://www.newyorktimes.com

Twenge, J. M., Haidt, J., Lozano, J., & Cummins, K. S. (2022). Specification curve analysis shows that social media use is linked to poor mental health, especially among girls. *Acta Psychologica, 224*, 103512. https://doi.org/10.1016/j.actpsy.2022.103512

University of MN Extension Service. (2022). *Teens and social media use.* Minneapolis, MN. https://www.extension.umn.edu

Vannucci, A., Simpson, E. G., Gagnon, S., & Ohannessian, C. M. (2020). Social media use and risky behaviors in adolescents: A meta-analysis. *Journal of Adolescence, 79*, 258–274. https://doi.org/10.1016/j.adolescence.2020.01.014

Wikipedia. (2022, May 12). Social media. *Wikipedia.* https://en.wikipedia.org

Young, E. (2017, April 20). *New survey reveals Snapchat and Instagram are the most popular social media platforms among young American teens.* www.apnorc.org

Chapter 2

Social Media and Special Populations of Youth

Marjorie Hogan, MD

SOCIAL MEDIA AND SPECIAL POPULATIONS

Social media are probably at their prosocial best for identified special populations of youth; those facing headwinds over and above the maelstrom that is adolescence may find information, support, and affirmation in a safe and creative online environment. Of course, at the same time, connection with family, peers, and community in real-time are aspirations for a healthy journey through adolescence.

LGBTQ+ Teenagers

For over a decade, researchers have published data confirming the benefits of social media presence for LGBTQ+ youth (Lucero, 2017; McInroy et al., 2019; Berger et al., 2021). LGBTQ (lesbian, gay, bisexual, transgender, and queer) is a wide accepted acronym referring to sexual and gender minority identities and people (McInroy & Craig, 2015). A teen lays claim to "who I am" in many spheres of existence, including sexual orientation and gender identity, as well as place in the family, the peer group, school, interests, approach to the present and future. For LGBTQ+ youth, because of family, societal, media, social, and political headwinds, this journey to claiming and affirming identity—and place in the world—is fraught with challenge. In the lives of LGBTQ+ youth, disapproval and rejection are not uncommon. Social media communities may offer essential support, education, and affirmation for many LGBTQ+ youth.

Adolescents are adopting social media at an earlier age, with YouTube, Instagram, and Snapchat surpassing Facebook as the most popular social media websites (Anderson & Jiang, 2018).

Charmaraman and colleagues report in 2021 that 97 percent of LGBTQ teens (age thirteen to seventeen years) use at least one social media website (Charmaraman et al., 2021). A qualitative survey in 2021 found Instagram, Facebook, Twitter, TikTok, and Snapchat as most-used social media sites for LGBTQ youth (Berger et al., 2021; Hanckel & Chandra, 2021).

LGBTQ+ youth, and their straight peers, seek identity, connectedness, and affirmation on social media. However, for the former group, "these web-based opportunities are particularly critical sources of risk and resilience . . . given the disproportionate risks and limited access to social support they face in other contexts, such as home, school, and community" (Craig et al., 2015). Similarly, Lucero surveyed multiply marginalized LGBTQ youth, finding that over 68 percent of this group preferred communicating through social media (rather than in offline settings) since social media provided safe space for communicating and exploring identity (Lucero, 2017).

Craig and colleagues in 2021 created the Social Media Benefits Scale and surveyed over 6,000 LGBTQ+ teens about their perception of (and experience with) a variety of social media platforms. Social media emerged as a generally positive force in the lives of these teens with benefits including (Craig et al., 2021):

- the opportunity to explore and practice disclosing their emerging identities,
- a chance to "control and rehearse their social interactions,"
- ability to access identity-specific resources.

LGBQT+ teens not only sought support and role models for themselves in a safe space, but with time and comfort, teens may "engage in sharing LGBTQ+ content and participate in educating and supporting other LGBTQ+ people within their online networks" (Craig et al., 2021). A 2021 cross-sectional study of young sexual minority youth found them significantly more likely than heterosexual youth "to report that they join web-based communities to feel less alone." "They created close-knit web-based peer communities (distinct from family) for self-expression and amelioration of loneliness" (Charmaraman et al., 2021). An earlier study by Craig et al. was on the power of positive media representations of LGBTQ youth to decrease negative experiences and enhance self-esteem. Four themes emerged in this 2015 study of resilience-building through social media: "coping through escapism; feeling stronger; fighting back; and finding and fostering community" (Craig et al., 2015).

For transgender youth specifically, social media offers the aforementioned benefits, but also "transgender participants were able to access information and role models that remained largely inaccessible in their offline lives. Most transgender participants were also able to develop a community of transgender people online, who were able to provide relevant support, resources, and medical information" (McInroy & Craig, 2015). A 2020 qualitative study from a Midwestern gender clinic also found that social media offered transgender youth peer-based emotional support and informational guidance about health decisions (including educating other people in their lives). "Participants also referenced negative experiences, including harassment and exclusionary behavior online" (Selkie et al., 2020).

A study of trans youth in the United Kingdom found that "trans youth find a diverse range of online culture meaningful to their understanding of themselves and their world" (Jensen, 2017) and that social media sites may be conducive to community formation and peer discourse. Our current political environment makes online affirmation and support even more important.

Social media sites also provide information about mental health concerns for sexual minority teens. A 2018 study found that 76 percent LGBTQ youth (versus 32 percent non-LGBTQ youth) sought information online about depression. Similarly, 75 percent and 68 percent of LGBTQ youth have looked for information about anxiety or stress, respectively, nearly double their straight peers (Rideout et al., 2018). LGBTQ+ teens, in a recent qualitative study, report that social media can be protective against common mental health issues (Berger et al., 2021). One study found that LGBTQ+ teens reported more loneliness and social isolation, and tragically, self-harm attempts were twice as likely compared to heterosexual peers. Nearly 40 percent reported having no one to talk with about sexual identity. There was "an overarching pattern of social media use that had a tone of social isolation (e.g., not responding when friends share good or bad news and being less motivated to share what they enjoy with friends)" (Charmaraman et al., 2021).

As has been mentioned, social media come with both risks and benefits. A qualitative 2021 study from Australia interviewed LGBTQ+ teens finding themes and corresponding subthemes describing their social media experience. These teens used social media platforms for "for identity, relationships and support"; however, social media also remain[ed] "a virtual setting for discrimination" (Berger et al., 2021). Despite the study's finding of positive social support through social media participation for LGBTQ+ teens, "participants also reported experiences of discrimination, including homophobia, transphobia and racism . . . indicating that these virtual 'safe spaces' are not immune to facilitating negative interactions" (Berger et al., 2021). The figure from this study graphically lays out the duality of potential benefit and harm from social media for LGBTQ+ youth.

The mission of GLAAD Media Institute, an organization created over thirty-five years ago, is to create and ensure inclusive and safe media environments for all users, across many domains, including film, television, advertising, family-focused media, video games, sports, political media, and journalism. Now, social media platforms are also a focus. GLAAD created the Social Media Safety Index (SMSI) to generate industry accountability (13), specifically finding that "the unique needs of LGBTQ people have largely been invisible or fall low on the priority list" (GLAAD, 2021). The SMSI not only documents negative and unsafe representations of LGBTQ people (in a specific fashion for the major social media platforms), but also establishes a roadmap for change aimed at specific media entities. The roadmap may include recommendations for content moderation, fact-checking, and mitigating misinformation, changing algorithms, hiring LGBTQ employees, and more. With growing awareness across social media sites of hate speech and harassment directed at LGBTQ people, as well as misinformation, GLAAD has created resources to assist users and industry leaders to mitigate harmful content (GLAAD, 2021).

Navigating adolescence skillfully presents real challenges for all teens, but certainly more so for marginalized LGBTQ youth. Uncertain of finding family, neighborhood, and peer support, teens' online activity may provide that very essential community, especially for those further marginalized living in rural areas, conservative states, or being members of other underserved groups. Social media sites serve a variety of functions for savvy LGBTQ teens, including opportunities to explore and cement sexual and/or gender identity; to meet like-minded peers; to practice engaging socially with others; to seek and learn accurate information about health and other topical issues; to provide education and support to others; to curate and produce media; and, to be entertained. "We may argue that software has the potential to aid the transformation of the teenager's bedroom into a civic and community space; a space for peer education, activism and enculturation" (Jensen, 2017).

At the same time, risks still remain. Different platforms are rife with messages of homophobia, transphobia, and racism. Cyberbullying is an ever-present possibility, and LGBTQ teens may not have support to avoid and challenge these risks. Parents and other caring adults, including teachers and other family and community members, should stay vigilant to the vulnerability of all adolescents engaging with social media sites, but particularly to already marginalized LGBTQ youth. Figure 2.1 illustrates how social media may provide benefit and/or harm to these young people (Berger et al., 2021).

(used with permission from Berger MN, Taba M, Marino JL, Lim MSC, Cooper SC, Lewis L, Albury K, Chung KSK, Bateson D, Skinner SR). Social media's role in support networks among LGBTQ adolescents: a qualitative study. *Sex Health.* 2021 Nov;18(5):421–431. doi: 10.1071/SH21110 (PMID: 34706814).

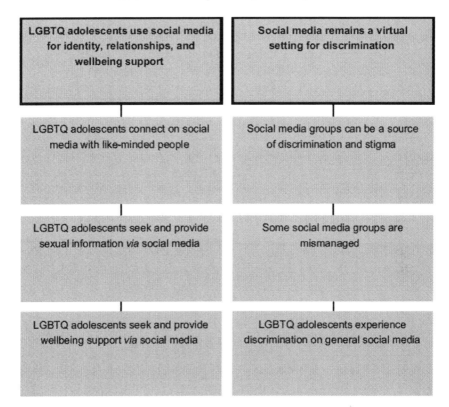

Figure 2.1 Social Media's Role in Support Networks among LGBTQ Adolescents: A Qualitative Study. *Source*: Used with permission from Berger MN, Taba M, Marino JL, Lim MSC, Cooper SC, Lewis L, Albury K, Chung KSK, Bateson D, Skinner SR. Social media's role in support networks among LGBTQ adolescents: A qualitative study. *Sex Health*. 2021 Nov;18(5):421–431. doi: 10.1071/SH21110. PMID: 34706814.

Teens with ASD/Autism

The most recent edition of the DSM revised its definition of autism spectrum disorder to include the following:

"(A) persistent deficits in social communication and social interaction and (B) restricted, repetitive patterns of behavior, interests, or activities" (American Psychiatric Association, 2013).

Thus, children and youth diagnosed with autism spectrum disorder may find joining a peer group, participating in activities with peers, and communicating (with peers and adults) to be challenging. These youth also often have problems interpreting nonverbal communication, managing sensory input, and tolerating changing situations.

Studies of adults with autism spectrum disorder find that social media use confers generally beneficial outcomes. One study found that Facebook used in moderation "may enhance well-being and may be a protective factor against secondary mental health concerns common" in adults with ASD (Ward et al., 2018). A 2021 survey of adults with autism found the highest users of social media faced greater risk of cyber-bullying; however, "self-esteem was positively correlated with feelings of belonging to an online community and negatively correlated with feelings of being ignored on social network sites and chat rooms" (Triantafyllopoulou et al., 2021). The authors found that in-person encounters for adults with autism may be difficult, given their challenges with communication and reading nonverbal cues. Therefore, use of social media may be an accessible alternative for social relationships and loneliness mitigation.

Youth with ASD use media as much or more than their peers. However, a 2012 study found "the majority of youths with ASD (64.2%) spent most of their free time using non-social media (television, video games), while only 13.2% spent time on social media (email, Internet chatting). Compared with other disability groups (speech/language, learning, intellectual), rates of non-social media use were higher among the ASD group and rates of social media use were lower" (Mazurek et al., 2012).

A systematic review of forty-seven studies of media use by youth with autism also found screen media (television, video games) to be the most common leisure activity. Social media was far less commonly used when compared with youth without ASD (Stiller & Mößle, 2018). This systematic review called for more studies on the functionality of screen time for youth with ASD as only a few studies examined using media for enjoyment, as a social bridge, for avoidance of social interaction, or as compensation for a lack of friends.

In contrast, Alhujaili and colleagues surveyed youth with and without autism spectrum disorder, finding that the two groups used social media at about the same rate, but for different reasons (Alhujaili et al., 2022). Youth with ASD preferred YouTube in this sample and chose this site for entertainment, rather than for social interactions, seemingly because YouTube is more passive and doesn't require any efforts at social interaction like Snapchat. Although evidence suggests that interactive social media could assist youth with autism by teaching and modeling social skills, this study suggests that these youth are not accessing social media for this purpose (Alhujaili et al., 2022).

Facebook features many groups on its site focusing on youth with autism and their families. To understand how this community uses Facebook, researchers conducted a content analysis of 500 such groups (Abel et al., 2019). The majority (60 percent) of the groups provided emotional support through the narrative sharing of stories, as well as an opportunity to share information and advice with peers. Other groups focused on a social community, advocacy, options for treatments, and sales or fundraising. That many youth with autism and their families use Facebook in this study demonstrates the power of social connection and support for this community. Intuitively, potential benefits of social media involvement for youth with autism are exciting, including the use of social media to reduce feelings of isolation and increase a sense of community (Abel et al., 2019):

- Interactions via social media can be easier than face-to-face interactions.
- ASD individuals can find personally relevant resources and information when involved in online communities.
- Access to support groups may be available.
- Youth may connect to others with shared interests.
- Social media may provide opportunities to practice interactions to improve real-life communication skills (Wood & Dalli, 2018).

Kuo and colleagues surveyed ninety-one youth with ASD and their parents and found those adolescents with ASD who accessed social networking websites or received emails from peers "reported more positive friendships" (Kuo et al., 2014). Another study found social media use to be "significantly associated with high friendship quality" for adolescents with ASD, which was influenced by the adolescents anxiety levels (van Schalkwyk et al., 2019). Van Schalkwyk et al. see an opportunity to enhance social communication and peer engagement for adolescents with ASD through social media use. They call for the development of "interventions which help adolescents not only spend time on these platforms, but find ways to be effectively and actively engaged. Adults should be aware of the potential for high anxiety to undermine the benefits of social media use in youth with ASD" (van Schalkwyk et al., 2019).

In 2022, Zhu and colleagues published results of a study cocreating social media sites specifically for youth with ASD and their parents on the creative team. Findings suggest that this creative process (in a safe, familiar environment) allowed youth to use self-efficacy skills through the design process, and that parents, community groups, and peers could, in fact, work effectively to engage youth with ASD on a social network (Zhu et al., 2022).

Youth on the autism spectrum face challenges when visiting social media sites, some similar to non-ASD peers, but others unique. For all teens, impulsive texts/e-mails/posts risk adverse consequences and may leave a permanent digital footprint. However, problems can occur with communication deficits, desire for solitary play, restricted interests, sensory and executive function difficulties, and conflict with parents (Lane & Radesky, 2019).

In 2016, Dunckley summarized the unique neurobiology in people with ASD leading to brain vulnerabilities related to screen time, including social media (Dunckley, 2016). For example, youth with autism are known to have sleep disturbances; screen time may disrupt restorative REM sleep, and, otherwise, exacerbate bedtime and overnight sleep problems. Youth with autism tend to have challenges with arousal regulation and managing stress response. The well-documented social and communication problems noted in those with ASD (less eye contact, difficulty interpreting facial expressions and body language, and decreased empathy) are skills further hindered by screen use. Dunckley also notes anxiety, decreased attention skills, and mood disorders as potential risks for this group of media users (Dunckley, 2016).

Lane and Radesky reviewed the use of media in the lives of children with ASD, again noting the prevalence of television and video games, but exploring the implications of more complex, individualized, and interactive digital media (Lane & Radesky, 2019). See Table.

ASD-related characteristic	Media characteristic
Social communication deficits	More predictable content and interactivity than interpreting human social information
Restricted interests	Highly personalized, restricted content; endless supply of videos/information
Sensory differences (seeking and avoidant)	High visual or auditory salience, gamified interactive elements, satisfying sensory experience
Executive functioning/self-monitoring weaknesses	Persuasive design acts on more subconscious habits/rewards; media multitasking is more common in young adults with executive functioning weaknesses
Low satisfaction from other activities	Highly rewarding; provides feeling of power and control/wish fulfillment
High parenting stress	Effective behavior reinforcement tool in keeping children occupied and calm; portable and instantly accessible (with both positive and negative consequences, depending on displacement of other activities or parent coping)

Source: Table used with permission from Rebecca Lane, MD, Jenny Radesky, MD. Digital Media and Autism Spectrum Disorders: Review of Evidence, Theoretical Concerns, and Opportunities for Intervention. *J Dev Behav Ped*. 2019 Jun; 40(5): 364–368

Wise use of platforms as a tool for enhancing social interaction and language skills through connection with family and peers is an opportunity. As well, parents and others adults should access the power of digital media for entertainment and education for their children (e.g., teaching computer coding, foreign languages, or creating videos or art) (Lane & Radesky, 2019). As suggested in American Academy of Pediatrics (AAP) materials, media (in any form) are best viewed with a parent who can turn any media offering into a learning experience through discussion, modeling, and reinforcement. Obviously, more research is needed.

Specific risks to all teen social media users, but amplified for those with ASD, include (Wood & Dalli, 2018; Lane and Radesky, 2019):

- Perseveration
- Limitations of social opportunities
- Exposure to inappropriate material
- Exposure to predators
- Cyberbullying
- Social anxiety/unreasonable expectations
- Extensive "secret rules"

A 2021 study of seventy-eight adults with autism analyzed social media use, experience with cyberbullying, and self-esteem. Participants were frequent users of social media and 37 percent reported being victims of cyberbullying. "The feeling of belonging in an online community had a positive effect on participants, promoting feelings of pride and usefulness, whereas being ignored on social media elevated feelings of worthlessness and negativity" (Triantafyllopoulou et al., 2021). A study of youth with ASD found high rates of engaging in cyberbullying and experiencing cyber-victimization; these were associated with anxiety, but interestingly, not depression (Holfeld et al., 2019).

Youth with ASD benefit from adult guidance in seeking online communities, especially considering safety concerns and the overwhelming number of extant social media sites. A 2018 presentation laid out helpful advice for parents and youth with ASD as guidelines for healthy social media use (Wood & Dalli, 2018):

- Choose the right time of day (to protect good sleep habits);
- Monitor your child's account and delete any hurtful, unsafe comments;
- Monitor and filter friends and contacts, within reason;
- Allow your child to have privacy about their conditions and help determine what they should share;
- Explore many social platforms until your child find the one.

University College London (UCL) funded and published an excellent "Rough Guide to Social Media Use for Teens with Autism," with an animated, engaging edition for both youth and parents (Autistic Adolescents' Use of Social Media, 2022).

Clearly, social media use offers potential benefits for youth on the autism spectrum, but more research is indicated and adult guidance for appropriate and safe use is wise. For all teens, building a community of friends is an essential task, and while in-person encounters and activities are important, engagement on social media platforms could enhance the lives of youth with ASD.

Youth with Chronic Illness

Countless children and teens suffer from chronic illnesses, with varying severity, prognoses, and impacts on physical, mental, and emotional health (Low & Manias, 2019; Kelleher et al., 2020). Intuitively, social media could ideally offer forums for youth to meet peers dealing with such diseases. They could meet not only for support and friendship but also to share resources, questions, and stories. As well, youth could use social media sites to connect with care teams about disease management—on their own terms, time, and with some control. "Living with a [chronic illness] can lead to feelings of stigmatization and emotional pain due to being different from peers" (Kelleher et al., 2020), as well as a variety of stresses such as financial, emotional, isolation, and missing out on typical adolescent activities.

Kohut et al. published a qualitative, descriptive study of teens with chronic illness (Kohut et al., 2018). These youth frequently accessed health-related websites. Ideally, these sites would provide both specific, accurate health information and a community of peers for support.

Reviewing a database of articles, Berkanish et al. investigated the use of technology to connect to adolescents with chronic disease and facilitate peer support. Whether discussion boards, Facebook groups, or video-conferencing platforms, results demonstrated "the feasibility, acceptability, and beneficial effects of telehealth and other digital interventions on quality of life, symptom management, medication adherence, and satisfaction outcomes among children and adolescents" (Berkanish et al., 2022).

Low and Manias reviewed studies of varying design to determine the role of technology-based tools in assisting adolescents and young adults (AYAs) with chronic illnesses to transition to adult health care. Youth with a variety of illnesses wanted accurate information on diverse, but relevant topics, including anxiety and stress management, dealing with insurance, and having social relationships (Low & Manias, 2019). And receiving disease-specific information—including management of the illness, transition tips, research updates, and supportive peer support—was important in the studies reviewed. Some AYAs such as online discussions or chat rooms are wary of privacy issues, but generally youth with chronic illness preferred an online support group to ease isolation and allow networking with peers. Low and Manias conclude that "providing AYAs an age-appropriate, reliable condition-specific resource, which can be accessed anywhere, is the very first step in supporting them to becoming resourceful independent adults managing their own care" (2019).

A 2019 study using focus groups of young people with type I diabetes found that social media could theoretically facilitate "improved communication outside of clinic visits to optimize diabetes management, independence in diabetes self-management, connection to other youth with diabetes for additional diabetes support, and delivery of more timely and personalized care" (Malik et al., 2019). The authors see social media as a potential tool for youth with type 1 diabetes, keeping professionalism and privacy in mind.

Szeto and colleagues surveyed youth with inflammatory bowel disease (IBD) in 2018 about their Internet habits. Only a small percentage (17 percent) accessed information about IBD, despite daily Internet use. Only 16 percent of these youth connected with peers with IBD. The authors surmise that "targeted education and skill building could be helpful for these youth as interest in mobile apps was reported" (Szeto et al., 2018). Social media is a potentially powerful tool in assisting teens with IBD with management, education, and monitoring of their chronic disease.

A 2020 cross-sectional pilot study of AYA with a variety of connective tissue disorders found that while social media use was nearly ubiquitous, a majority did not use social media to discuss their condition or know someone online with a similar condition, although these youth expressed interest in finding peers with the same condition (Kelleher et al., 2020).

In Italy, another cross-section study of youth with a variety of serious, chronic illnesses found that nearly 98 percent valued sharing their experiences with friends on social media and nearly 95 percent sought information about their specific diseases on the Internet, notably the prognosis of the illness. More than 70 percent of youth in the study "perceived dependence on their parents as the most negative aspect of having a chronic disease" and nearly every youth surveyed did not want medical care providers on social media sites. When youth are experiencing acute symptoms of their chronic illness, time spent on social media platforms more than doubled for this group, from an average of hours to 11 hours daily (DeNardi et al., 2020).

Many youth are surviving cancer today with enhanced treatment methods and surveillance. Youth with cancer may not experience normal young adult milestones or may view the future through a negative lens (DeClercq et al., 2020).

A small study of young people with cancer found social media to promote positive identity and social development. "Specifically, social media provide spaces to negotiate body image and sense of self, to manage peer relationships, to reclaim control and independence, and to maintain normalcy"

(Daniels et al., 2021), no small feat for this vulnerable group undergoing cancer treatment.

De Clercq and colleagues did a scoping review of articles exploring the role of social media in the context of providing optimal care for young people with cancer (DeClercq et al., 2020). Several benefits were identified, including the following:

- "A kind of 'life-line' to the outside world";
- Factual source on cancer diagnosis, treatments, and side effects, depending on the timeline for individual AYAs;
- Source of behavioral encouragement, such as exercise, nutrition, treatment reminders;
- Source of support (both peer and professional) when off-line friends and family are not available or sufficient.

All youth with chronic illness using social media logically face many challenges—privacy, confidentiality, security, and observing professional boundaries, although the benefits may outweigh the concerns (DeClercq et al., 2020). A 2022 study of AYA with cancer found social media presence generally beneficial; however, about one in six reported cyberbullying (Daniels et al., 2021). Thus, social media could be extremely helpful (Virella Perez et al., 2021), but must provide accurate, accessible information about specific diseases and a responsible community of online support (Kohl et al., 2018)

Youth Experiencing Marginalization or Underrepresentation

All adolescents must navigate the challenging years between childhood and adulthood encountering similar tasks and challenges, but with different strengths, support systems, opportunity, and access. These developmental tasks include establishing and gaining comfort with identity, connecting with a peer group and finding comfort and affirmation in social spaces, and finding one's place in family, school, and community. Some youth encounter significant barriers to successfully completing the journey through adolescence smoothly and successfully, whether by virtue of race or ethnicity, immigrant status, whether they are urban or rural, educational status, sexual or gender identification, educational opportunity, or socioeconomic status. Social media may play a pivotal role in the lives of these marginalized, underrepresented teens. Social media may allow underrepresented youth to draw on resources and support from peers, make connections with people who may be helpful, and identify resources not available offline (Brough et al., 2020).

Native American or Indigenous youth historically have faced discrimination, lack of educational opportunity, and a plethora of health risks (Rice et al., 2016; Craig Rushing et al., 2018). Technology-based health interventions are emerging as an effective strategy for promoting health and well-being in American Indian/Alaskan Native (AI/AN) populations (Stephens et al., 2020). A survey in 2018 of nearly 700 AI/AN youth found that 78 percent had regular access to a smartphone, and 92 percent could access the Internet daily or weekly, including to obtain health information (Craig Rushing et al., 2018). Searches included information about relationships, birth control or pregnancy, and depression, among other topics. Respondents felt more comfortable with an online exchange, rather than turning to peers, a clinician, or a trusted adult or parent.

As a result, the "We R Native" service was designed and implemented, including a website (www.weRnative.org), text messaging service, and sites on social media platforms (Facebook, Twitter, Instagram, YouTube). We R Native offers community service grants, contests, and an approachable "Ask Auntie" column (Craig Rushing et al., 2018). We R Native emphasizes healthy behaviors, sexual health, positive mental health, connections to Indigenous LGBTQ communities, and encouragement about STEM education. The service promotes positive identity, accent on culture and tradition, and community: "We are a comprehensive health resource for Native youth, by Native youth, providing content and stories about the topics that matter most to them. We strive to promote holistic health and positive growth in our local communities and nation at large" (Craig Rushing et al., 2018). The services are monitored for metrics and outcomes.

A systematic review involving Indigenous youth in Australia found that social media "provides opportunities [for these youth] to feel a sense of power and control over their own identities and communities" (Rice et al., 2016). The authors reviewed and evaluated twenty-two studies of this population of youth and identified the following:

- Social media platforms, such as Facebook and YouTube, allow Indigenous youth "to connect with, affirm and give voice to their Indigenous identities" (Rice et al., 2016).
- Social media allows youth agency how to seek information and how to communicate.
- The visual and narrative Indigenous culture can be shared providing opportunities for transmitting intergenerational knowledge.
- Indigenous families and communities may be widespread, and social media may allow Indigenous young people to stay connected with family and friends, promoting well-being. Although some families do not have access to technology in the home, many have mobile phones (Rice et al., 2016).
- Social media use may provide an opportunity to improve educational and health outcomes, the latter including smoking cessation and sexual health.

This systematic review also identified some negative associations with social media, such as cyberbullying and cyber racism. The authors call for more research into how to purposefully engage Indigenous youth with social media programs to optimize health, identity, and well-being (Rice et al., 2016).

An innovative 2020 follow-up study in Portland (an extension of the We R Native) recruited over 1,000 AI/AN teens to receive either BRAVE text messages ("designed to improve mental health, help-seeking skills, and promote cultural pride and resilience") or STEM-based text messages ("designed to elevate and re-affirm Native voices in science, technology, engineering, math and medicine") (Stephens et al., 2020). The groups then received the other texts. The engagement of the youth in bidirectional, dynamic texting suggests that social media—with culturally relevant images and language—will be an important strategy in optimizing health of Indigenous youth. The authors concluded that health information delivered and discussed through social media sites "can amplify and reinforce healthy social norms and cultural values, teach suicide warning signs, prepare youth to initiate difficult conversations with peers and trusted adults, encourage youth to access mental health resources, destigmatize mental health, and connect youth to trusted adults" (Stephens et al., 2020).

A 2022 study recruited 100 teen males from each of the four groups experiencing marginalization: participants identified as Black, East/SE Asian, Indigenous, or Latinx. These youth were queried on demographics, social media use habits, social media group diversity, social media racial justice engagement, social media racial discrimination, mental health symptoms, and risky behaviors (Tao & Fisher, 2022). Almost all (94 percent) participants had experienced vicarious social media racial discrimination and 79 percent had experienced personal social media racial discrimination. Black youth were most likely to report racial discrimination. Time spent on social media was associated with racial discrimination, symptoms of depression and anxiety, and alcohol and drug use problems (Tao & Fisher, 2022).

Another group of youth experiencing marginalization is immigrant and refugee youth. Whether from Central America in recent years, Southeast Asia over several decades, Africa and the Middle East, or escaping from current war in their countries of origin, these teens face huge obstacles in this country. Learning a new language, entering the school system, finding a community of friends, and facing racism and other forms of discrimination, the teens are also grappling with grief, often PTSD, and parents as vulnerable as they are. Documentation status often looms as a major issue.

The potential role of social media is being examined in the lives of these marginalized teens. A 2020 study from Norway using focus groups found that social media platforms offered opportunities for health promotion messages and allowed recently arrived youth to establish identities and discuss social control. Yet "social media consists of social codes and structures, and unequal accessibility, like other social arenas" (Speldnaes & Agdal, 2020), so barriers still exist.

Researchers at George Washington University described the Adelante Youth Ambassador program for immigrant Latino youth as a pilot attempt to use digital media to reduce health risks such as substance use, sexual risk, and violence (Barrett et al., 2017). Latino youth ambassadors designed and created videos with positive, preventive health messages for dissemination and discussion with peers. The program measured changes in confidence (positive identity), civic engagement, connection with the community, and connection with peers as a result of the social media outreach. For Latino immigrant youth, Barrett et al. concluded that a multistrategy approach that included in-person activities, social marketing and media advocacy campaigns, and prosocial videos offered a positive way to engage them in activities that encourage health promotion and positive identity. Specifically, participants demonstrated a nearly 70 percent increase in civic engagement, an over 50 percent increase in connection with the community, and slight increase in positive identity (Barrett et al., 2017).

Youth experiencing homelessness (YEH)—estimated at 4.2 million young people under the age of twenty-five—face daunting challenges. About 700,000 of these youth are unaccompanied, so without parent or family (National Conference of State Legislatures, 2022). YEH report substance abuse/misuse (29 percent), mental health problems (69 percent), and being part of the foster care (33 percent) or juvenile justice system (50 percent) (Barman-Adhikari & Craddock, 2019; National Conference of State Legislatures, 2022; Chapin Hall, 2022). Additional risks include being a victim of physical or sexual assault. Many YEH identify as LGBTQ youth, twice as many as their heterosexual peers. Lack of a diploma or GED appears to be the major correlate for youth homelessness (National Conference of State Legislatures, 2022; Chapin Hall, 2022).

A 2014 study of 201 YEH found that despite having less regular access to the Internet, YEH used the Internet to access information and resources, entertain themselves, and to socialize. The most common habits were checking e-mail (64 percent) and checking social networking websites (56 percent) (Rice & Barman-Adhikari, 2014). Clearly homeless youth need to socialize just like housed youth. The authors found that youth who remained connected to friends and family were more likely to look for jobs and housing resources online. They concluded that social media can serve as positive and powerful resources for YEH in meeting their social and resource-seeking needs (Rice & Barman-Adhikari, 2014).

A qualitative study in 2017 questioned youth experiencing marginalization in depth about their experiences, positive and negative, on social media, again confirming that these teens use the Internet and social media platforms often (minimum use was once daily) and for many reasons (Regan, 2017). They accessed social media to contact peers and family—to maintain close offline relationships—or for entertainment purposes. In their interviews, "reflections included awareness that social media functioned as a tool to meet new people and provided an opportunity to bridge connections in a way that has never before been seen. They also acknowledged that social media functioned as a resource to learn from others, as well as to provide and receive support" (Regan, 2017). Interestingly, participants recognized that some populations are more vulnerable on social media, specifically children and seniors, and the youth called for rules to govern social media and provide protection and support.

In a survey of eight-seven, YEH found that 56 percent accessed the Internet at least once a day, while 86 percent reported at least weekly use. The study participants used smart phones or public computers for online access. Entertainment activities online decreased, while Internet activities became more goal-oriented as these teens used online time for basic needs such as housing, food, and employment (VonHoltz et al., 2018). Study participants used the Internet to seek a range of health information, including acute illnesses, child development, alternative medicine and remedies, cancer, exercise, nutrition and calories, provider and hospital contact information, and STIs. They were interested in being involved in the development of a website or app that would aggregate resources and address relevant concerns. The authors stress the importance of digital inclusion for all homeless young people (VonHoltz et al., 2018).

Many marginalized adolescents exist in society today. Social media can offer opportunities for them to engage in community, national, or global dialogue about important issues that affect them, and at the same time, build advocacy skills by using an accessible platform that is familiar to them (Barrett et al., 2017). Social media's easy access and popularity allows for prevention efforts and intervention driven by youth engagement and owner-ship of products and strategies. Studies have shown how social media can allow youth who experience social marginalization to draw on resources from members of the networks to which they belong, make connections with people who may be helpful to them, and gain access to resources they might not have offline. Clearly, high-quality, inclusive, creative research is needed.

Social Media and Sexual Health

Sexual health in adolescents remains a crucial concern today. This group accounts for a large proportion of STIs diagnosed, and although rates have fallen, teen pregnancy impacts the lives of young parents and their children (Teadt et al., 2020; Cornelius et al., 2019; Fowler et al., 2021).

Adolescents use various social media platforms avidly; each new survey finds high user rates, often many times daily (Common Sense Media, 2022). Cell phone access for teens is nearly ubiquitous. Many youth seek and find health information online, from diet and nutrition to intimate questions about sex, sexuality, gender, STIs, and pregnancy.

During the pandemic, both young patients and their providers found technology instrumental in seeking and delivering health care. Many clinic systems have safe, easy-to-use platforms for patients. Privacy remains a concern for teens—if a provider is speaking to a teen, are there others within earshot? One-on-one conversations between provider and teen offer a new means of accessing health care, and social media broadly offers opportunity to not only connect with youth but also to disseminate information, reminders, and prompts about safe behaviors to a wider audience:

- For example, a 2017 study of 250 African-American and Latino youth found that those receiving safe sexual health information via social media were two times more likely to use contraception or condoms at last intercourse (but those receiving sexual health information by word-of-mouth were four times more likely to use protection). Those youth receiving sexual health messages elsewhere (from school, parents, or traditional media) were not more likely to use contraception or condoms (Stevens et al., 2017). The authors suggest that social media may function as a "super peer" (Strasburger, et al., 2014), establishing sexual risk reduction norms and transmitting them to others. Clearly, this potential influence demands accurate, attractive information for adolescent social media users.
- A study of over 400 Native American and Alaskan Native youth tested the effectiveness of a social media intervention (via text messages) to encourage condom use and STI/HIV testing. Surveys after intervention showed improvement not only in attitude about condom use but also in condom use behavior and STI/HIV testing intention. The improvement was maintained at least three months postintervention (Yay et al., 2018).
- A three-month-long social media intervention with the "overarching goal to improve adolescents' knowledge about HPV and HPV vaccination" (Ortiz et al., 2018) found that participants engaging with the social media campaign improved knowledge about HPV and HPV vaccination when compared with a control group, even discussing their new knowledge with others. However, this knowledge did not translate to a significant increase in vaccination rates. The authors suggest that for motivated adolescents, receiving health information via social media offers potential opportunities for health care providers to engage them.

- In a randomized clinical trial of nearly 300 teens with PID, those in the "technology enhanced" intervention group experienced decreases in STIs over time and were significantly more likely to present for follow-up care. Those in the intervention group received text messages daily for two weeks followed by booster messages with reminders about taking medications; this group also had a community nurse visit (Trent et al., 2019).
- Because of the high rate of teen STIs in both the United States and Botswana, a 2019 focus group study analyzed social media use of teens in both countries and their perceptions of safer sex interventions delivered via mobile phone. Although youth in the two countries frequented different social media sites, all "were receptive to the idea of using social media for the delivery of safer sex information. And why not? This is how they live. This is how they learn" (Cornelius et al., 2019).
- A scoping review (sixteen studies) of the role of new media platforms in promoting safe sex and reducing sexual risk among African American youth found promise in the technology (2). The review found new media to be a feasible method of delivery sexual health promotion with high levels of participation by the African American youth. Several interventions identified were effective in changing attitudes and behaviors related to sexual health from negative to more positive (Teadt et al., 2020). Participants noted that social media are attractive because it is anonymous, convenient, and accessible. Youth also were more likely to seek health care resources after seeing health information online.

A 2020 needs assessment study (using both a survey and focus groups) sought to identify "social media utilization practices, strategies to effectively engage teens on social media, and recommendations for teen health promotion on social media" (Plaisime et al., 2020). The study reviewed and confirmed previous work, that both female and male teens primarily use social media to connect with family and friends, while males tended to use social media to seek information. Both high- and low-frequency users utilize social media for health information on nutrition, fitness, and sexual health. Sensitive issues such as drugs or sex are more popular to be discussed online than in person (Plaisime et al., 2020). Participants liked relatable posts—targeted to the teen audience, humorous, entertaining, and motivational.

The innovative sexually transmitted infections and sexual health (STASH) intervention trains influential student peers to disseminate positive and safe sexual health messages both via social media and in-person conversation (Hirvonen et al., 2021; Mitchell et al., 2021). A feasibility study in six schools in Scotland in 2021 found the intervention to be a generally positive experience for peer supporters, students, and schools, although students noted privacy concerns and the stigma of sexual health discussion. Further implementation and evaluation are planned, including exploring how offline discussion and social media can work together (Hirvonen et al., 2021).

Fowler et al. evaluated 100 TikTok videos purporting to provide sexual health information (#sexeducation). It offers an anonymous way to access information about all sexual orientations and interest, topics that may not be discussed in school sex ed programs. This informal sex education curriculum is beyond the oversight of parents, teachers, and health care providers. The likelihood of at least some misinformation occurring raises concerns, however (Fowler et al., 2021).

Condom use education on YouTube is successful with young Africa American males if promoted by someone "respected in the community or someone famous" or if the segment included where condoms were available (for free or for purchase) (Burns et al., 2021). Another recent study showed that messages conveyed through traditional communication channels about condom use and first-time HIV testing were important for at-risk Latino/a youth, but social media (Clarke et al., 2021).

If social media can provide accurate, accessible, appealing sexual health information for teens, no matter the gender, race, sexual orientation, identity, age, this knowledge may influence attitude, intention, and ultimately sexual behaviors. "Due to their remarkable efficiency in disseminating information to large groups, SNSs have the potential to be a powerful tool" in sex education, decision-making, and healthier behaviors (Plaisime et al., 2021). Obviously, the accuracy of the sexual health information and the appeal to youth through relevance, humor, and salience matters.

Final Thoughts

Social media in all their glory, complexity, angst, and innovation are here to stay, continually evolving and challenging all users, children through seniors. Will we (and our teens and tweens) reap the benefits of connectivity, creativity, and inclusion, or succumb to yet another "vast wasteland," a term coined by Newt Minow decades ago referring to the specter of television? (Minow, 1961).

REFERENCES

Abel, S., Machin, T., & Brownlow, C. (2019). Support, socialise and advocate: An exploration of the stated purposes of Facebook autism groups. *Res Autism Spectrum Disord, 61*, 10–21. https://doi.org/10.1016/j.rasd.2019.01.009

Alhujaili, N., Platt, E., Khalid-Khan, S., & Groll, D. (2022). Comparison of social media use among adolescents with autism spectrum disorder and non-ASD adolescents. *Adolesc Health Med Ther, 13*, 15–21. https://doi:10.2147/AHMT.S344591

American Psychiatric Association. (2013). *Diagnostic and statistical manual of mental disorders* (5th ed.). https://doi.org/10.1176/appi.books.9780890425596

Anderson, M. A., & Jiang, J. (2018). *Teens, social media and technology.* Washington, DC: Pew Research Center. https://www.pewresearch.org

Autistic Adolescents' Use of Social Media. (2022). *Rough guide to social media use for teens with autism.* UCL Grand Challenges Adolescent Lives, Award 156425. https:www.ucl.ac.uk

Barman-Adhikari, A., & Craddock, J. (2019). How we can leverage social networks, tech to help homeless young. *Youth Today.* Center for Sustainable Journalism at Kennesaw State University. https://www.youthtoday.org

Barrett, N., Villalba, R., Andrade, E., Beltran, A., & Evans, W. D. (2017). Adelante ambassadors: Using digital media to facilitate community engagement and risk-prevention for Latino youth. *J Youth Dev*, *12*(4). https://doi.org/10.5195/jyd.2017.513

Berger, M. N., Taba, M., Marino, J. L., Lim, M. S. C., Cooper, S. C., Lewis, L., Albury, K., Chung, K. S. K., Bateson, D., & Skinner, S. R. (2021). Social media's role in support networks among LGBTQ adolescents: A qualitative study. *Sex Health*, *18*(5), 421–431. https://doi.org/10.1071/SH21110

Berkanish, P., Pan, S., Viola, A., Rademaker, Q., & Devine, K. A. (2022). Technology based peer support interventions for adolescents with chronic illness: A systematic review. *J Clin Psychol Med Settings.* Advance online publication. https://doi.org/10.1007/s10880-022-09853-0

Brough, M., Literat, I., & Skin, A. (2020). "Good social media?": Underrepresented youth perspectives on the ethical and equitable design of social media platforms. *AoIR Sel Pap Internet Res.* Advance online publication. https://doi.org/10.1177/2056305120928488

Burns, J., Chakraborty, S., & Arnault, D. S. (2021). Social media preference and condom use behaviors: An analysis of digital spaces with young African American males. *Health Educ Behav*, *48*(2), 190–198. https://doi.org/10.1177/1090198121993043

Chapin Hall. (2022). *Voices of youth count: Understanding and ending youth homelessness.* Chicago, IL: University of Chicago. https://www.chapinhall.org

Charmaraman, L., Hodes, R., & Richer, A. M. (2021). Young sexual minority adolescent experiences of self-expression and isolation on social media: Cross-sectional survey study. *JMIR Ment Health*, *8*(9), e26207. https://doi.org/10.2196/26207

Clarke, R. D., Fernandez, S. B., Hospital, M., Wagner, E. F., & Wales, E. (2021). Getting their feet in the door: Communication cues to action for HIV testing and condom use behaviors among Hispanic/Latinx college students. *J Prim Prevent*, *42*, 331–341. https://doi.org/10.1007/s10935-020-00610-3

Common Sense Media. (2022). *The common sense census: Media use by tweens and teens.* San Francisco, CA: Common Sense. https://www.commonsensemedia.org

Cornelius, J. B., Whitaker-Brown, C., Neely, T., Kennedy, A., & Okra, F. (2019). Mobile phone, social media usage, and perceptions of delivering a social media safer sex intervention for adolescents: Results from two countries. *Adolesc Health Med Ther*, *10*, 29–37. https://doi.org/10.2147/AHMT.S185041

Craig, S. L., Eaton, A. D., McInroy, L. B., Vivian, W. Y., Leung, V. W. Y., & Krishnan, S. (2021). Can social media participation enhance LGBTQ+ youth well-being? Development of the social media benefits scale. *Social Media + Society*, January–March, 1–13.

Craig, S. L., McInroy, L., McCready, L. T., & Alaggia, R. (2015). Media: A catalyst for resilience in lesbian, gay, bisexual, transgender, and queer youth. *J LGBT Youth*, *12*, 254–275. https://doi.org/10.1080/19361653.2015.1040193

Craig Rushing, S. N., Stephens, D., & Ghost Dog, T. L. (2018). We R native: Harnessing the power of social media to promote AI/AN adolescent health. *J Adolesc Health*, *62*, S37–S140.

Daniels, S. R., Yang, C. C., Toohey, S. J., & Willard, V. W. (2021). Perspectives on social media from adolescents and young adults with cancer. *J Pediatr Oncol Nurs*, *38*(4), 225–232. https://doi.org/10.1177/1043454221992319

De Clercq, E., Rost, M., Gumy-Pause, F., Diesch, T., Espelli, V., & Elger, B. S. (2020). Moving beyond the friend-foe myth: A scoping review of the use of social media in adolescent and young adult oncology. *J Adolesc Young Adult Oncol*, *9*(5), 561–571. https://doi.org/10.1089/jayao.2019.0168

De Nardi, L., Trombetta, A., Ghirardo, S., Genovese, M. R. L., Barbi, E., & Taucar, V. (2020). Adolescents with chronic disease and social media: A cross-sectional study. *Arch Dis Child*, *105*(8), 744–748. https://doi.org/10.1136/archdischild-2019-317996

Dunckley, V. L. (2016). Autism and screen time: Special brains, special risks. *Psych Today*. https://www.psychologytoday.com

Fowler, L. R., Schoen, L., Smith, H. S., & Morain, S. R. (2021). Sex education on TikTok: A content analysis of themes. *Health Promot Pract*. Advance online publication. https://doi.org/10.1177/15248399211031536

GLAAD. (2021). *Social media safety index*. New York, NY: GLAAD. https://www.glaad.org

Hanckel, B., & Chandra, S. (2021). *Social media insights from sexuality and gender diverse young people during COVID-19*. Sydney, Australia: Western Sydney University. https://www.doi.org/10.26183/kvg0-7s37

Hirvonen, M., Purcell, C., Elliott, L., Bailey, J. V., Simpson, S. A., McDaid, L., Moore, L., & Mitchell, K. R. (2021). Peer-to-peer sharing of social media messages on sexual health in a school-based intervention: Opportunities and challenges identified in the STASH feasibility trial. *J Med Internet Res*, *23*(2), e20898. https://doi.org/10.2196/20898

Holfeld, B., Stoesz, B., & Montgomery, J. (2019). Traditional and cyber bullying and victimization among youth with autism spectrum disorder: An investigation of the frequency, characteristics, and psychosocial correlates. *J Dev Disabilities*, *24*, 61–76.

Jensen, O. (2017). Trans youth and social media: Moving between counterpublics and the wider web. *Gender Place Cult*, *24*(11), 1–16. https://www.doi.org/10.1080/0966369X.2017.1396204

Kelleher, E. F., Giampietro, P. F., & Moreno, M. A. (2020). Social media use among young adults with connective tissue disorders: Cross-sectional pilot study. *JMIR Pediatr Parent*, *3*(2), e16367. https://doi.org/10.2196/16367

Kohut, S. A., LeBlanc, C., O'Leary, K., McPherson, A. C., McCarthy, E., Nguyen, C., & Stinson, J. (2018). The internet as a source of support for youth with chronic conditions: A qualitative study. *Child Care Health Dev*, *44*(2), 212–220. https://doi.org/10.1111/cch.12535

Kuo, M. H., Orsmond, G. I., Coster, W. J., & Cohn, E. S. (2014). Media use among adolescents with autism spectrum disorder. *Autism*, *18*(8), 914–923. https://doi.org/10.1177/1362361313497832

Lane, R. & Radesky, J. (2019). Digital media and autism spectrum disorders: Review of evidence, theoretical concerns, and opportunities for intervention. *J Dev Behav Pediatr*, *40*(5), 364–368. https://doi.org/10.1097/DBP.0000000000000664

Low, J. K., & Manias, E. (2019). Use of technology-based tools to support adolescents and young adults with chronic disease: Systematic review and meta-analysis. *JMIR Mhealth, 7*(7), e12042. https://doi.org/10.2196/12042

Lucero, L. (2017). Safe spaces in online places: Social media and LGBTQ youth. *Multicult Educ Rev, 9*(2), 117–128.

Malik, F. S., Panlasigui, N., Gritton, J., Gill, H., Yi-Frazier, J. P., & Moreno, M. A. (2019). Adolescent perspectives on the use of social media to support type 1 diabetes management: Focus group study. *J Med Internet Res*, *21*(6), e12149. https://doi.org/10.2196/12149

Mazurek, M. O., Shattuck, P. T., Wagner, M., & Cooper, B. P. (2012). Prevalence and correlates of screen-based media use among youths with autism spectrum disorders. *J Autism Dev Disord*, *42*, 1757–1767. https://doi.org/10.1007/s10803-011-1413-8

McInroy, L. B., & Craig, S. L. (2015). Transgender representation in offline and online media: LGBTQ youth perspectives. *J Hum Behav Soc Environ*, *25*, 606–617. https://www.doi.org/10.1080/10911359.2014.995392

McInroy, L. B., Craig, S. L., & Leung, V. W. Y. (2019). Platforms and patterns for practice: LGBTQ+ youths' use of information and communication technologies. *Child Adolesc Soc Work J*, *36*(5), 507–520. https://doi.org/10.1007/s10560-018-0577-x

Minow, N. N. (1961). *Television and the public interest.* National Association of Public Broadcasters. https://www.americanrhetoric.com

Mitchell, K. R., Purcell, C., Simpson, S. A., Broccatelli, C., Bailey, J. V., Barry, S. J. E., Elliott, L., Forsyth, R., Hunter, R., McCann, M., McDaid, L., Wetherall, K., & Moore, L. (2021). Feasibility study of peer-led and school-based social network intervention (STASH) to promote adolescent sexual health. *Pilot Feas Stud*, *7*(1):125. https://doi.org/10.1186/s40814-021-00835-x

National Conference of State Legislatures. (2022). *Youth homelessness overview.* Washington, D.C.: NCSL. https://www.ncsl.org

Ortiz, R. R., Shafer, A., Cates, J., & Coyne-Beasley, T. (2018). Development and evaluation of a social media health intervention to improve adolescents' knowledge about and vaccination against the human papillomavirus. *Glob Pediatr Health*, *5*. https://doi.org/10.1177/2333794X18777918

Plaisime, M., Robertson-James, C., Mejia, L., Nunez, A., Wolf, J., & Reels, S. (2020). Social media and teens: A needs assessment exploring the potential role of social media in promoting health. *Social Media Soc, 6*(1). https://doi.org/10.1177/2056305119886025

Regan, K. A. (2017). Socially marginalized youths' experiences with social media and its impact on their relationships. *Electronic Thesis and Dissertation Repository*, p. 4476. https://ir.lib.uwo.ca/etd/4476

Reuman, H., Kerr, K., Sidani, J., Felker, J., Escobar-Viera, C., Shensa, A., & Maurer, S. H. (2022). Living in an online world: Social media experiences of adolescents and young adults with cancer. *Pediatr Blood Cancer*, 69(6), e29666. https:// doi .org/10.1002/pbc.29666

Rice, E., & Barman-Adhikari, A. (2014). Internet and social media use as a resource among homeless youth. *J Comput Mediat Commun*, 19(2), 232–247. https://doi.org /10.1111/jcc4.12038

Rice, E. S., Haynes, E., Royce, P. L., & Thompson, S. C. (2016). Social media and digital technology use among Indigenous young people in Australia: A literature review. *Int J Equity Health*, 15, article 81. https://doi.org/10.1186/s12939-016-0366-0

Rideout, V., Fox, S., & Well Being Trust. (2018). Digital health practices, social media use, and mental well-being among teens and young adults in the U.S. *Articles, Abstracts, and Reports*. https://digitalcommons.psjhealth.org/publications/1093

Selkie, E., Adkins, V., Masters, E., Bajpai, A., & Shumer, D. (2020). Transgender adolescents' uses of social media for social support. *J Adolesc Health*, 66, 275–280. https://doi.org/10.1016/j.jadohealth.2019.08.011

Spjeldnaes, I. O., & Agdal, R. (2020). "A room of our own": Social media use amongst youth with immigrant background in Norway. *Eur J Pub Health*, 30, 5. https://doi.org/10.1093/eurpub/ckaa166.389

Stephens, D., Peterson, R., Singer, M., Johnson, J., Craig Rushing, S., & Kelley, A. (2020). Recruiting and engaging American Indian and Alaska Native teens and young adults in a SMS help-seeking intervention: Lessons learned from the BRAVE study. *Int J Environ Res Public Health*, 7(24), 9437. https://doi.org/10.3390/ijerph17249437

Stevens, R., Gilliard-Matthews, S., Duane, J., Todhunter-Reid, A., Brawner, B., & Stewart, J. (2017). Social media use and sexual risk reduction behavior among minority youth: Seeking safe sex information. *Nurs Res*, 66(5), 368–377. https:// doi.org/10.1097/NNR.0000000000000237

Stiller, A. & Mößle, T. (2018). Media use among children and adolescents with autism spectrum disorder: A systematic review. *J Autism Dev Disord*, 5, 227–242. https://doi.org/10.1007/s40489-018-0135-7

Strasburger, V. C., Wilson, B. J., & Jordan, A. B. (2014). *Children, adolescents and the media*. Thousand Oaks, CA: Sage Publishing.

Szeto, W., van der Bent, A., Petty, C. R., Reich, J., Farraye, F., & Fishman, L. N. (2018). Use of social media for health-related tasks by adolescents with inflammatory bowel disease: A step in the pathway of transition. *Inflamm Bowel Dis*, 24(6), 1114–1122. https://doi.org/10.1093/ibd/izy021

Tao, X., & Fisher, C. (2022). Exposure to social media racial discrimination and mental health among adolescents of color. *J Youth Adolesc*, 51(1), 30–44. https:// doi.org/10.1007/s10964-021-01514-z

Teadt, S., Burns, J. C., Montgomery, T. M., & Darbes, L. (2020). African American adolescents and young adults, new media, and sexual health: Scoping review. *JMIR Mhealth Uhealth*, 8(10), E19459. https:// doi.org/10.2196/19459

Trent, M., Perin, J., Gaydos, C. A., Anders, J., Chung, S. E., Saeed, L. T., Rowell, J., Huettner, S., Rothman, R., & Butz, A. (2019). Efficacy of a technology-enhanced community health nursing intervention vs standard of care for female adolescents and young adults with pelvic inflammatory disease: A randomized clinical trial. *JAMA, 2*(8), e198652. https://doi:10.1001/jamanetworkopen.2019.8652

Triantafyllopoulou, P., Clark-Hughes, C., & Langdon, P. E. (2021). Social media and cyber-bullying in autistic adults. *J Autism Dev Disord, 19*, 1–9. https:// doi.org/10 .1007/s10803-021-05361-6

van Schalkwyk, G. I., Marin, C. E., Ortiz, M., Rolison, M., Qayyum, Q., McPartland, J. C., Lebowitz, F. E., Volkmar, F. R., & Silverman, W. K. (2019). Social media use, friendship quality, and the moderating role of anxiety in adolescents with autism spectrum disorder. *J Autism Dev Disord, 47*(9), 2805–2813. https://doi.org /10.1007/s10803-017-3201-6

Virella Perez, Y. I., Medlow, S., Ho, J., & Steinbeck, K. (2019). Mobile and web-based apps that support self-management and transition in young people with chronic illness: Systematic review. *J Med Internet Res, 21*(11), e13579. https://doi .org/10.2196/13579

VonHoltz, L. A. H., Frasso, R., Golinkoff, J. M., Lozano, A. J., Hanlon, A., & Dowshen, N. (2018). Internet and social media access among youth experiencing homelessness: Mixed-methods study. *J Med Internet Res, 20*(5), e9306. https://doi .org/10.2196/jmir.9306

Ward, D. M., Dill-Shackleford, K. E., & Mazurek, M. O. (2018). Social media use and happiness in adults with autism spectrum disorder. *Cyberpsych Behav Soc Netw, 21*(3). https://doi.org/10.1089/cyber.2017.0331

Wood, T. & Dalli, M. (2018). Autism and social media presentation. Marie Dalli, Speech and Language Pathologist. Parent Training curriculum in the Syosset Central School District. Used with permission from Dr. Wood.

Yao, P., Fu, R., Craig Rushing, S., Stephens, D., Ash, J. S., & Eden, K. B. (2018). Texting 4 sexual health: Improving attitudes, intention, and behavior among American Indian and Alaska native youth. *Health Promot Pract, 19*(6), 833–843. https://doi.org/10.1177/1524839918761872

Zhu, R., Hardy, D., & Myers, T. (2022). Community led co-design of a social networking platform with adolescents with autism spectrum disorder. *J Autism Dev Disord, 52*(1). https://doi.org/10.1007/s10803-021-04918-9

Chapter 3

To Friend or Not to Friend

Helping Teachers Maintain Boundaries on Social Media

Susan Eva Porter, PhD, LCSW

A teacher affects eternity; he can never tell where his influence stops.

—Henry Adams

LIFE BEFORE DIGITAL TECHNOLOGY

Recall, if you can, the time before digital technology was omnipresent in education.

Back then—a long, long time ago—teaching was conducted only in person, and the best learning management system was a teacher's gradebook. There were no Power Point presentations, no emails from parents, and no YouTube videos distracting students from their homework. A Golden Age, of sorts, or certainly a simpler one.

I remember the precise moment I knew working in schools had changed forever due to digital technology. It was midway through the first decade of the century, maybe in 2005 or '06, and I was working as a school counselor at a K-12 school on the East Coast. As a counselor, I was used to dealing with the emotional vagaries of my students and to responding to them throughout the day. Teachers often referred students to my office, or students referred themselves; they dropped by for a chat, a quiet moment, or for help solving a problem.

On this memorable day, however, I received an e-mail from a parent. This was before I/We/Everyone spent the entire day on e-mail, and for the most part, my interactions with parents still happened over the phone or in person.

An e-mail from a parent during the day was a somewhat unusual occurrence at that time, and this one especially so.

> "I need you to check on my daughter," the parent wrote.
> "Immediately!"
> I was alarmed, to say the least, and kept reading.
> "My daughter just texted me that she had an argument with her friend, and you need to check on her right away!"

Because I hadn't received an e-mail like this before—where events were being reported in real time, and where a parent demanded that I act immediately—I responded as directed. I hurried to her daughter's classroom to assess the situation, only to find that her daughter was happily ensconced in her lessons.

By the time I returned to my office, there was another e-mail from the parent waiting in my inbox.

> "Never mind. Everything's fine!"

I can't remember if I felt relieved or not to get this second e-mail. I do remember, though, feeling like it was the end of the world as I knew it. My takeaway from that simple yet jarring e-mail exchange was that the boundaries between students and parents, and between parents and schools, were being obliterated. Digital technology was about to radically change the way I did my job, and even how I thought about myself as a professional. For me, this moment was the dividing line—the end of the technological stone age—and the beginning of a whole new world in schools.

And this was before social media hit the scene (Ortiz-Ospina, 2019).

SOCIAL MEDIA IS BORN

It was around this time that Facebook started to emerge as a thing. At the beginning, membership was limited to college students at select schools (this was when FB was characterized by exclusivity, not inclusivity), but there were thunderclouds on the horizon. After my e-mail exchange with the concerned parent, I started to pay more attention to what was happening out there, in the social media world, although I had no idea how soon, or how completely, it would infiltrate and change the lives of my students, and everyone's.

During the next few years I watched as the number of my students who used social media increased exponentially, to the point where it was rare to find a student that *didn't* connect to their peers in this way, and I also watched as social media became a place where adults connected. First Facebook was for (elite) college students, then it was for any college students, then it was for high school students, and then it was for the rest of us (Auxier and Anderson, 2022).

I believe this creep toward the whole world using social media has left those of us who work with students vulnerable in various ways. All of a sudden, over the course of a few years, teachers have gone from being with their students only during the school day to potentially being exposed to their students, and to what they are doing, and vice versa, 24/7.

This is a radical shift for the teaching profession, and it raises all kinds of questions about best practices for teachers on social media, such as is it possible for teachers to have healthy and appropriate connections online with their students? And if so, how much interaction should teachers have with their students online? How do teachers stay safe—that's right, safe—from the risks of getting too close or too exposed to students in the social media vortex? And, should teachers avoid connecting to students online altogether?

These are essential questions for all of us in the teaching profession to consider, but I don't hear most teachers/schools asking them. I believe we must pay close attention to how social media affects the relationships between children and adults in schools or we do ourselves and our students a great disservice. Using social media—even when teachers do not connect directly with their students—leaves every adult who works with children vulnerable

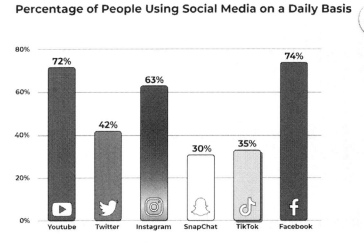

Figure 3.1 Percentage of People Using Social Media on a Daily Basis. *Source*: Auxier and Anderson, 2022

in many ways, and I believe every teacher, coach, administrator, and support personnel should be educated as to how.

And it all comes down to one thing.

Boundaries.

SOCIAL MEDIA—OBLITERATING BOUNDARIES

What social media does—and its intended purpose—is to dissolve boundaries (Gashler, 2019). Social media allows us to connect instantly with people across the room, across generations, and across the world. This boundary-obliterating technology rewards us for connecting with as many people as possible, many more than we could ever do in person, and for sharing things about ourselves that we might never share in a one-on-one conversation.

And, in fact, sharing isn't really the appropriate term for what we're doing on social media; it's more like parallel play. You do your thing and I do mine, and we do it alongside each other in a digital sandbox.

At first, when social media was an emerging phenomenon, I was mostly concerned about the effect of this boundary-defying technology would have on students. What were the downsides of young people living their lives online, of exposing themselves to strangers? Would they live to regret an impulsive tweet or a compromising photo?

I would (and still do) harp endlessly about the risks my students take by exposing certain aspects of their lives online, and how an impulsive decision to post a comment or picture can come back to haunt them (*think college admissions!* I say ominously). Approximately none of my students ever listen to my doomsday predictions, and I have come to accept that I sound like an old man on the porch when I talk about social media to kids, shaking my proverbial cane at the neighborhood kids who dart across my lawn.

While I still caution students to be careful about what they post on social media, I have given up being a maniac. Of course, I am still concerned for them, and of course, I still try to educate them about the risks of posting certain things, but I no longer beat the doomsday drum. At least not with my students.

With teachers, on the other hand, it's a different story.

TEACHERS AND SOCIAL MEDIA

I'm going to turn back the clock again, to the early days of social media, and to the fateful moment when I realized that teachers and school staff are playing with fire by not considering the impact their digital footprint can have on their students and their careers.

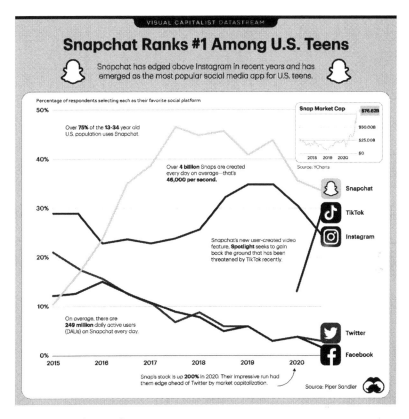

Figure 3.2 Snapchat Ranks #1 Among US Teens.

Did you hear about Sally? One of my colleagues said to me, in a nonwhisper whisper.

It was the mid-2000s, and we were in the teachers' lounge, probably eating lunch.

No. I replied. What happened?

I could sense the concern in my colleague's voice, and soon a small group of fellow teachers had gathered around.

A student saw her MySpace page and now, well, she's in talking to the principal.

Yikes, another colleague chimed in. That sounds ominous.

It is, confirmed the first colleague, although it was unclear to the rest of us why. She saw the perplexed looks on our faces.

Polyamory, she said, by way of explanation.

We all looked at each other in confusion.

With pictures, she added.

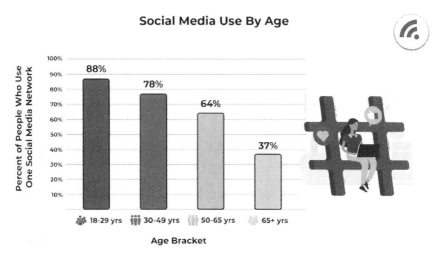

Figure 3.3   Social Media Use by Age.

The colleague in question had apparently posted information about her relationship status and romantic behavior online, which is exactly what people do on social media, but what she hadn't considered was that some of her students might be exposed to this information and find it interesting, and then report it to their parents, who then reported it to the school.

Back then, this was somewhat scandalous, both in terms of the content (many of us had to look up *polyamory*) and also because it seemed transgressive to many of us—we didn't know social media could be used for this kind of disclosure. Fast forward a decade and I think we'd all agree that such a posting is neither scandalous nor transgressive, but that doesn't mean we shouldn't be concerned as teachers about our online presence.

THERE'S NO SUCH THING AS PRIVACY ONLINE

I tell teachers to start with the assumption that everything they post on social media will be seen by their students (and their students' parents) and to act accordingly. To most people this is obvious, but it doesn't stop many teachers from behaving as though it isn't. I can't tell you how many teachers I know who post pictures of themselves drinking, smoking, partially clothed, doing drugs, looking unprofessional and foolish, spouting extreme political views, and doing all kinds of things that they'd never want their students to know about.

Take Jenna, for instance.

Jenna worked at a small high school where she had contact with every single student. She was part of the support team and worked closely with the entire student body. She also used hallucinogenic drugs frequently on the weekends, and posted about it. Often, Jenna was seen by the students as "cool," and her recreational and after-hours activities underscored this image for them, but their parents didn't think Jenna's behavior was so cool when they found out about it. Which of course they did.

Most schools have something in the Employee Handbook about not engaging in behavior that could tarnish the name of the school, often referred to as a "morals clause," and Jenna's behavior would certainly fall under this category. But let's imagine that Jenna worked at a school that didn't have such a requirement, and that she had free rein to post whatever she wanted to without fear of reprisal from her employer.

Would posting images of her engaging in illicit behavior still be a problem?

Yes, and here's why.

WHAT STUDENTS NEED FROM TEACHERS

Almost none of us entered the teaching profession because we were interested in raising other people's children. Rather, we loved our subject matter, loved working with kids, and loved the idea of making a difference in the world. These are all laudable reasons for wanting to teach. But the reality is teachers spend more time with children than parents do, and it's fair to say that teachers spend as much time serving as role models as anything else.

Before I continue, let me assure you that I am not here to moralize about how teachers should live their lives. Great teachers come in all shapes and sizes, metaphorically speaking, and there is no recipe for what kind of person will be an effective teacher. That said, there is one ingredient students need more than anything else from teachers in order to learn. They need them to be grown-ups.

So what's the definition of a grown-up? Well, it's not just someone who has reached a certain chronological age. That's an adult, and being an adult—when you can legally vote and drink and rent a car—does not in any way mean that you're a grown-up. You can be fifty years old and still be irresponsible and childish and selfish, and this is what I call being a grown-older (Porter, 2009).

There are plenty of grown-olders out there, and by and large, they don't make great teachers, in large measure because they don't understand what students need from them, or if they do they don't care. And now that social media has blurred the boundaries between teachers and students, students need their teachers to be grown-ups more than ever.

WHAT GROWN-UPS DO FOR STUDENTS

Here are some things grown-up teachers do for their students:

- They put their students first. This means that when they are in the class-room, a grown-up teacher recognizes that their job is to teach and to make sure their students learn. And when they post something online, a grown-up teacher takes into consideration that their students could see it, and in doing so have much more information about their teacher than they can handle.
- Grown-up teachers understand that a power differential exists between themselves and their students, and that it never should be ignored (Manke, 1997). Before posting something online, grown-up teachers ask themselves whether they would reveal this information directly to their students, and if not, then they don't post it.
- Grown-up teachers recognize that it is only, and always, their responsibility to maintain the essential boundary between themselves and their students. It is never a student's job to keep a boundary between themselves and their teacher, or to manage something their teacher posts online that they find disturbing.
- Finally, grown-up teachers understand that they can never be friends with their students—never. They recognize the important distinction between being friendly with students and being friends, and they never confuse the two.

TO FRIEND OR NOT TO FRIEND—GUIDELINES
FOR TEACHERS USING SOCIAL MEDIA

One of the hazards of using social media for teachers is the premise that we're all equal when we're sharing social media spaces. All of our opinions can be expressed, all of our voices can be heard, and for the most part, there's very little oversight in the process. This is all fine and well except when we factor in any of our students' needs, in which case it makes using social media a potential minefield.

The following are some guidelines for teachers to consider in an effort to protect themselves and their students online:

- Consider not using social media at all. Most teachers won't make this choice, but if you've ever looked for an excuse to get off of social media, here it is.
- If you do use social media, consider creating accounts that use names that are not easily searchable by your students (although, always assume a tech savvy student can track you down).

- Set boundaries and say no—do not accept friend requests from current students (and be cautious about accepting requests from former students). If you need help with this, and your school doesn't already have a policy in place, ask the administration to consider creating a policy restricting the kind of connections teachers can have with students online.
- If you are determined to ignore the above advice, create an account that is only for connecting with students. Why you'd want to do this is another question, but at least you can safeguard the information that you post to this account.
- Do not post anything on social media that you do not want to be read by your students and their parents, and then by your principal.
- Tell your supervisor immediately if you have any concerns about interactions with students online. Do not operate in isolation.

This last guideline is critical for teachers to heed if you choose to connect with students online. Being on social media means you will inevitably be exposed to some student behavior and circumstances that may require a response. Make sure you understand your school's policy about mandated reporting, for instance, and share with your supervisor any disturbing or harmful student behavior you are exposed to online.

MAKING A DIFFERENCE

You became a teacher to help students, to make a difference. One of the biggest differences you can make in your students' lives, apart from teaching them, is to be cautious about how you behave online. You will never get the Teacher of the Year Award for setting boundaries and being a grown-up, but you will have given your students what they need.

And in this way, your work will become eternal.

SUGGESTED READING

Feinstein, S. (2009). *Inside the teenage brain*. Lantham, MD: Rowman & Littlefield Education.
Jensen, F. E., and Nutt, A. E. (2015). *The teenage brain: A neuroscientist's survival guide to raising adolescents and young adults*. New York: HarperCollins.

Lythcott-Haims, J. (2015). *How to raise an adult.* New York: Henry Holt and Company.

Porter, S. E. (2009). *Relating to adolescents: Educators in a teenage world.* Lanham, MD: Rowman & Littlefield Education.

Siegel, D. J. (2013) *Brainstorm: The power and purpose of the teenage brain.* New York: Jeremy P. Tarcher/Penguin.

Strauch, B. (2003). *The primal teen.* New York: Doubleday.

REFERENCES

Ali, A. (2020, December 16). *Snapchat: The most popular social media among U.S. teens.* Visual Capitalist. Retrieved March 15, 2022, from https://www.visualcapitalist.com/snapchat-the-most-popular-social-media-among-us-teens/

Auxier, B., & Anderson, M. (2022, January 31). *Social media use in 2021.* Pew Research Center: Internet, Science & Tech. Retrieved March 15, 2022, from https://www.pewresearch.org/internet/2021/04/07/social-media-use-in-2021/

Gashler, K. (2019, February 21). *A new order: Controlling the boundaries of social media.* CALS. Retrieved March 3, 2022, from https://cals.cornell.edu/news/new-order-controlling-boundaries-social-media

Manke, M. (1997). *Classroom power relations.* London: Routledge.

Ortiz-Ospina, E. (2019, September 18). *The rise of social media.* Our World in Data. Retrieved March 15, 2022, from https://ourworldindata.org/rise-of-social-media

Porter, S. E. (2009). *Relating to adolescents: Educators in a teenage world* (pp. 39–64). Lantham, MD: Rowman & Littlefield Education.

Surprising Social Media Statistics—The 2022 Edition. (2022). BroadbandSearch. Net. Retrieved 3–15, from https://www.broadbandsearch.net/blog/social-media-facts-statistics

Chapter 4

Cyberbullying among Youth

Dorothy L. Espelage, Cagil Torgal, Alberto Valido,
Luz E. Robinson, and Graceson L. Clements

Youth today are born into a world where digital media has become integral to their daily lives. Many interact with screens in early childhood, with children five years and younger being the fastest growing digital media users.[1] Significant advancements in technology have created an environment that allows youth to interact in ways that are considerably different from face-to-face interactions.[2]

Smartphones and social networking sites (SNS) such as Twitter, Instagram, Snapchat, and TikTok have become a core part of daily social interactions, and many adolescents have friends they only met online.[3,4]

Notably, researchers highlight that youth's digital environment and what they experience in these spaces shape their identity development.[5,6,7] For example, while SNS may help youth build community through frequent connections with their peers, it may also result in feelings of isolation when they encounter conflicts or challenging interactions with peers.[5] Thus, it is critical to monitor how youth's digital experiences are associated with well-being and adverse outcomes.

Over the last two decades, there has been an increasing interest in identifying threats to safety in online spaces.[8] The dynamics and unique properties of the interactions in digital media and concerns regarding online safety have attracted attention from scholars in various fields.[5]

Not only is cyberbullying quite prevalent among adolescents, but cyberbullying perpetration and victimization have been associated with deleterious academic and social outcomes, including decreased academic achievement and increased depression and suicide.[9,10] This chapter discusses cyberbullying characteristics and briefly highlights the latest research findings and implications for schools.

WHAT IS CYBERBULLYING?

Cyberbullying is defined as "willful and repeated harm inflicted through the use of computers, cell phones, or other electronic devices."[11] In the early stages of cyberbullying research, cyberbullying was considered an extension of bullying; however, given the unique nature of cyberspace, it is now conceptualized as a different form of aggressive behavior.[12]

Similar to face-to-face bullying, cyberbullying may also take different forms. For example, it may appear as posting hurtful comments on someone's photo in SNS, sending hurtful messages, or even intentionally excluding individuals in group chats.[13] Another platform where cyberbullying commonly occurs is in online multiplayer games where players can interact with each other using audio or video.[14] Yet, adolescents may perceive online aggressive behavior as a part of "gaming culture" rather than considering it as cyberbullying.[15]

Similar to face-to-face bullying, cyberbullying may also occur privately or publicly.[13] However, due to the nature of online spaces, the audience of public cyberbullying victimization may be much more extensive than face-to-face bullying.[12]

In a recent qualitative study that investigates children and adolescents' perceptions of cyberbullying, participants emphasized the publicity aspect of cyberbullying and how it may exacerbate the negative impact of victimization.[16] For example, they suggested that the possibility of bystanders sharing and reposting harmful posts increases the distress caused by the incident.

ONLINE DISINHIBITION

Researchers have been trying to understand better the factors that shape people's experiences in the digital world by using different theories to explain people's perceptions and behaviors in online spaces.[17,18] More specifically, it is critical to understand how the nature of online spaces exacerbates the intensity of actions and the harm that is done as a consequence of these actions.

One explanation of the mechanisms that enable individuals to act differently in online platforms is the online disinhibition effect.[19,20] Suler (2004) argues that individuals may feel less concerned about the propriety of their actions as they can choose to be anonymous and invisible in their online interactions.[20]

Further, individuals are more likely to minimize the impact of their actions in online spaces as they do not face any immediate negative consequences for most of their harmful actions. Moreover, as most online interactions lack important social cues, such as facial expressions, and individuals are not there to physically see the aftermath of their actions, they are less likely to empathize with others.

PREVALENCE OF CYBERBULLYING
IN THE UNITED STATES

In a recent survey that investigated the prevalence of cyberbullying in middle school aged children in the United States, researchers found that 21 percent of participants reported being involved in cyberbullying as a perpetrator, a victim, or a bystander.[21] Furthermore, according to the 2019 Youth Risk Behavior Survey ($N = 10,309$; 50.1 percent girls), 16 percent of high school students reported experiencing cyberbullying in the previous year.[22]

Some populations are also found to be more susceptible to being cyberbullying victims or perpetrators.[23] While there are mixed findings regarding differences based on sex, in their recent study, Patchin and Hinduja (2021)[21] suggest that boys are more likely to report being perpetrators of cyberbullying than girls. Another nationally representative survey suggests that girls are twice as likely to be victims of cyberbullying compared to boys.[24]

Furthermore, similar to traditional bullying, individuals with disabilities were found to be more prone to being cyberbullying victims.[9] Similarly, youth with neurodevelopmental disorders (e.g., attention deficit and hyperactivity disorder, autism spectrum disorders) were found to be more likely to be involved in cyberbullying as victims or perpetrators.[25]

Sexual and gender minorities are also at risk for cyberbullying involvement. Research findings highlight that while there is a wide range of prevalence of involvement (10.5–71.3 percent), LGBTQ youth are more likely to be targeted in cyberbullying incidents compared to heterosexual and cisgender youth.[26]

Given the changes associated with the COVID-19 pandemic, children and youth became even more immersed in online spaces. The COVID-19 pandemic resulted in limited in-person activities increasing the likelihood of interaction in online spaces. Additionally, the changes in the school system and transition to fully online content made digital involvement mandatory. As there is a well-established positive association between digital media use and cyberbullying, this increase in online involvement raised concerns about the prevalence of cyberbullying.[27]

While there is a paucity of research specifically examining the impact of COVID-19 on youth's cyberbullying experiences in the United States, the current research findings are mixed. For example, in a study conducted by an organization that uses artificial intelligence for online hate speech detection, researchers examined a multitude of online platforms (e.g., websites, SNS, and gaming platforms) for hate speech and online toxicity. Results of their study revealed a 70 percent elevation in cyberbullying and hateful comments among youth across various online mediums.[28]

On the other hand, in a study that used Google search intensity as their measure of the prevalence of cyberbullying, Bacher-Hicks et al. (2022)[29] examined the Google search intensity of the terms "cyberbullying," "school bullying," and "bullying" in both national and state levels. They suggest that search intensity reflects people's likelihood of looking for resources for bullying, which may indicate they have experienced bullying.

Their findings showed that in a regular prepandemic academic school year, search intensity of these terms peaks at the beginning of the school year, starts declining throughout the year, and is at the lowest point in summer. These findings were supported by self-report and behavioral measures of bullying and cyberbullying, where researchers observed similar trends.

When they looked at the search intensity of the same terms during the pandemic, overall, they observed a significant decline compared to prepandemic search intensity. They also found that the search intensity was higher in states with higher in-person education rates than in states with higher rates of remote education. While the research about the repercussions of the pandemic is still in its early stages, findings may still shed light on risk and protective factors of cyberbullying.

RISK FACTORS OF CYBERBULLYING
VICTIMIZATION AND PERPETRATION

Adolescents' involvement in cyberbullying is complex and likely influenced by multiple factors, including the individual, family, peer group, and community context.[30] Findings show that the risk of cyberbullying varies according to grade level. Like face-to-face bullying, cyberbullying increases and peaks during middle school and the transition to high school.[31,32]

However, some studies have found elevated rates among elementary students, a trend that may increase as digital media technologies become more widely available to younger students.[33,34] Higher cyberbullying involvement during middle school and high school may be explained by the growing importance of the peer context and the perceived social benefits of engaging in cyberbullying behavior.

Cyberbullying perpetration often occurs in the presence of online bystanders who may reinforce peer social norms supportive of harmful online behavior.[35] Social norm theory posits that perceived social norms in the peer group strongly influence adolescents' beliefs and behaviors.[36] Adolescents may perceive that their friends are supportive and approve of cyberbullying, leading them to higher perpetration to obtain the social gains associated with that behavior. There is evidence to support this theory, as research has found cyberbullying perpetration to be longitudinally associated with higher peer perceived popularity.[37]

These findings suggest that adolescents may be motivated to engage in cyberbullying to gain social status among their peers. When a cyberbullying comment is liked, commented on, and reposted, adolescents are given an audience that is likely to reinforce the social status of the perpetrator while multiplying the harm done to the victim. As such, cyberbullying magnifies the power imbalance between the perpetrator and victim by providing social gains for the perpetrator while isolating and marginalizing the victim.[37]

Perpetrators may also use cyberbullying to reinforce other forms of aggression such as homophobic name-calling, gender or sexual stereotypes, sexual harassment, or other forms of bias-based bullying. Although most studies have focused on heterosexual adolescents, a systematic literature review reveals that LGBTQ youth are vulnerable to higher online and offline victimization rates.

The review found evidence that LGBTQ youth are more likely to experience anonymous forms of cyberbullying compared to their heterosexual peers[38,39] and that cyberbullying is ranked as one of the highest forms of prejudice affecting LGBTQ youth, with rates between 28 percent and 49 percent.[40] Youth who do not conform to traditional gender roles are especially vulnerable to online harassment and humiliation.

In a study by GLSEN, cisgender nonheterosexual females, transgender youth, and youth who identified as "other" gender reported higher rates of cyberbullying victimization compared to youth who identified as cisgender gay or bisexual males.[26,41] Bisexual students have also shown elevated rates of cyberbullying victimization compared to youth identifying as other sexual minorities.[26,42]

There is a dearth of research on the experiences of bisexual youth and what may explain these disparities. These findings highlight the need for targeted programming efforts and further research to prevent cyberbullying victimization among sexual and gender expansive youth.

EFFORTS OF PREVENTION

Youth are increasingly connecting through diverse social communication platforms (e.g., TikTok, SnapChat, and Instagram). Efficacious cyberbullying prevention and intervention are imperative to the health and well-being of adolescents. Thus, various strategies have been developed, implemented, and evaluated, including school-based programs, parental involvement and support, and bystander training.

Numerous school-based programs have been developed and implemented to reduce cyberbullying involvement. Given the extensive literature and variability in program effectiveness, Polanin et al. (2021)[43] conducted a comprehensive systematic review and meta-analysis of school-based programs to decrease cyberbullying victimization and perpetration.

The review included published and unpublished literature and examined confirmatory and exploratory moderating factors. A total of 50 studies and 320 effect sizes across 45,371 participants were analyzed. Most studies were conducted outside of the United States, and only fourteen of the fifty studies included U.S. samples. The researchers identified seven programming categories to organize and synthesize the program components:

- (1) skill-building
- (2) curricula and prepared materials
- (3) psychoeducation
- (4) multimedia materials
- (5) training
- (6) school climate or school policy
- (7) group or individual targeted responses.

Approximately 80 percent of the programs evaluated included some form of skill-building, 67 percent included curricula or other prepackaged materials, and 65 percent included multimedia materials. The least common components were group or individual targeted responses, school climate or policy, and training. All studies were conducted within the last fifteen years, and the majority, thirty-six, over the previous five years.

The meta-analysis indicated that school-based prevention programs were effective at significantly reducing both cyberbullying perpetration and victimization. Interestingly, program effectiveness was slightly higher for perpetration compared to victimization. The researchers also estimated that the average program included in this review would have a 76 percent probability of decreasing cyberbullying perpetration and a 73 percent probability of reducing cyberbullying victimization.

Results from the confirmatory moderator analyses suggested that programs were more effective at preventing cyberbullying and traditional bullying when they targeted cyberbullying specifically rather than targeting violence in general. Notably and consistent with the literature, programs in the United States had a smaller effect size compared to programs in Europe. This finding may be explained by a collective research effort in Europe that began in 2008.

The intergovernmental framework for European Cooperation in Science and Technology (COST)[44] included twenty-eight European countries that coordinated nationally funded research in Europe on cyberbullying. The

COST collaboration was intended to decrease the fragmentation in European research efforts, increase research cooperation worldwide, and has led to the development of several prevention programs targeting cyberbullying. There is no known collaboration in North America, thus, the research on school-based programs for cyberbullying prevention is relatively limited.

Parents are critical to reducing adolescent risk-taking behaviors, yet growing access to different online spaces presents novel challenges to parents and their cyberbullying prevention efforts. Elsaesser et al. (2017)[45] conducted a systematic review of parents' role in preventing cyberbullying among adolescents. They included twenty-three articles, primarily cross-sectional studies, on the associations between parental warmth and parental monitoring on cyberbullying victimization and perpetration among adolescents.

The review found that parental warmth was consistently associated with lower cyberbullying victimization and perpetration across studies. In this review, parental warmth was consistently related to a lower risk for cyberbullying victimization and perpetration. Findings also indicated that for parental monitoring, strategies focused on parental control, such as restricting access to the Internet, appear to be weakly related to youth's involvement in cyberbullying victimization and perpetration.

In contrast, parental monitoring strategies that are more collaborative, such as evaluative mediation and co-use, were more closely connected to cyberbullying victimization and perpetration prevention; however, evidence suggests that the effectiveness of these practices varied by ethnicity and sex.

Only four studies examined the connection between parenting styles and cyberbullying. Empirical evidence suggests that an authoritative parenting style, which combines high levels of warmth and control, is associated with lower cyberbullying perpetration.

These findings emphasize the positive role of parents who work collaboratively with their adolescents to navigate the Internet safely, which is more likely to protect against cyberbullying involvement than imposing restrictions without input from the adolescent. Given that most studies were cross-sectional, causal inferences cannot be made, thus, parent involvement and cyberbullying behaviors warrant future longitudinal research.

As technology rapidly changes and new forms of communication emerge, adolescents will likely find ways around restrictions on platforms and websites. Language is fluid, and new words or meanings may need to be interpreted collaboratively. Thus, parents' willingness to communicate with their adolescents and collaborate on Internet use may be protective against cyberbullying involvement.

Cyber-bystanders include any individual who witnesses cyberbullying. Anyone online has the potential to be a cyber-bystander and offer a unique role as they can set norms and standards of the types of language to be used on different online platforms.[46] However, few studies have focused on cyber-bullying prevention programs targeting bystanders.

Torgal et al. (2021)[47] conducted a recent meta-analytic review synthesizing the impact of school-based cyberbullying prevention programs on promoting cyber-bystander prosocial intervention among K–12 students. The meta-analytic synthesis included nine studies and thirty-five effect sizes. Given the variability in program components, researchers organized interventions into four programming categories:

- (1) self-efficacy
- (2) empathy activation
- (3) digital materials
- (4) bystander training

Findings indicated that overall, the school-based cyberbullying prevention programs were not statistically significant in promoting cyber-bystander prosocial behaviors. However, moderator analyses suggested that programs incorporating an empathy activation component were associated with better program effectiveness in promoting prosocial cyber-bystander intervention.

CONCLUSION

Cyberbullying continues to be a serious public health concern and a priority for future research and prevention efforts. The use of digital media technology is likely to increase in the future as novel mediums of communication are developed, making cyberbullying an urgent concern for policymakers and legislators. The complex and multifaceted nature of cyberbullying requires a concerted effort from schools, parents, community members, legislators, and social media companies.

Prevention must happen at multiple levels, including better monitoring of cyberbullying and harmful content in social media posts, anti-cyberbullying policies in schools, school-based prevention programs, greater involvement of parents and families, and international cooperation.

Given the broad reach of cyberbullying, finding ways to increase cyber-bystander prosocial intervention should be a priority for future program development and research. Future research should also focus on preventing bias-based cyberbullying and the role of prejudice in online media. Additionally, research that examines the effects of cyberbullying among students with neurodevelopmental disorders is needed.

Similarly, research that examines the effect of COVID-19 shutdowns on cyberbullying will help scholars understand how to best address the needs of students that have been affected during the pandemic. Lastly, the frontiers of cyberbullying research should focus on the impact of new forms of technology such as interactions occurring through virtual reality platforms (e.g., Oculus VR), multiplayer online gaming, and popular social media apps such as TikTok and Snapchat, and other online technologies yet to be developed.[48]

NOTES

1. Rideout, Victoria, and Michael B. Robb. "The Common Sense census: Media use by kids age zero to eight." *Common Sense Media* 263 (2017): 283.

2. Castells, Manuel. "Communication, power and counter-power in the network society." *International Journal of Communication* 1, no. 1 (2007): 29.

3. Lenhart, A. "Teens, technology and friendships." Retrieved May 3, 2017. (2015).

4. Nesi, Jacqueline, Sophia Choukas-Bradley, and Mitchell J. Prinstein. "Transformation of adolescent peer relations in the social media context: Part 1—A theoretical framework and application to dyadic peer relationships." *Clinical Child and Family Psychology Review* 21, no. 3 (2018): 267–294.

5. Granic, Isabela, Hiromitsu Morita, and Hanneke Scholten. "Beyond screen time: Identity development in the digital age." *Psychological Inquiry* 31, no. 3 (2020): 195–223.

6. Subrahmanyam, Kaveri, and David Šmahel. *Digital youth: The role of media in development.*
   New York, NY: Springer, 2011.

7. Uhls, Yalda T., Nicole B. Ellison, and Kaveri Subrahmanyam. "Benefits and costs of social media in adolescence." *Pediatrics* 140, no. Supplement_2 (2017): S67–S70.

8. Tynes, Brendesha M. "Internet safety gone wild? Sacrificing the educational and psychosocial benefits of online social environments." *Journal of Adolescent Research* 22, no. 6 (2007): 575–584.

9. Kowalski, Robin M., and Allison Toth. "Cyberbullying among youth with and without disabilities." *Journal of Child & Adolescent Trauma* 11, no. 1 (2018): 7–15.

10. Polanin, Joshua R., Dorothy L. Espelage, Jennifer K. Grotpeter, Katherine Ingram, Laura Michaelson, Elizabeth Spinney, Alberto Valido, America El Sheikh, Cagil Torgal, and Luz Robinson. "A systematic review and meta-analysis of interventions to decrease cyberbullying perpetration and victimization." *Prevention Science* (2021): 1–16.

11. Hinduja, Sameer, and Justin W. Patchin. "Cyberbullying: An exploratory analysis of factors related to offending and victimization." *Deviant Behavior* 29, no. 2 (2008): 129–156.

12. Zych, Izabela, Rosario Ortega-Ruiz, and Rosario Del Rey. "Scientific research on bullying and cyberbullying: Where have we been and where are we going." *Aggression and Violent Behavior* 24 (2015): 188–198.

13. Englander, E., E. Donnerstein, R. Kowalski, C. A. Lin, and K. Parti. "Defining cyberbullying." *Pediatrics* 140, Suppl. 2 (2017): S148–S151.

14. Ballard, Mary Elizabeth, and Kelly Marie Welch. "Virtual warfare: Cyberbullying and cyber-victimization in MMOG play." *Games and Culture* 12, no. 5 (2017): 466–491.

15. McInroy, Lauren B., and Faye Mishna. "Cyberbullying on online gaming platforms for children and youth." *Child and Adolescent Social Work Journal* 34, no. 6 (2017): 597–607.

16. Leduc, Karissa, Pooja Megha Nagar, Oksana Caivano, and Victoria Talwar. "'The thing is, it follows you everywhere': Child and adolescent conceptions of cyberbullying." *Computers in Human Behavior* 130 (2022): 107180.

17. Ansary, Nadia S. "Cyberbullying: Concepts, theories, and correlates informing evidence-based best practices for prevention." *Aggression and Violent Behavior* 50 (2020): 101343.

18. Espelage, Dorothy L., Inalini A. Rao, and Rhonda G. Craven. "Theories of cyberbullying." In *Principles of cyberbullying research* (pp. 77–95). Routledge, 2012.

19. Huang, Chiao Ling, Sining Zhang, and Shu Ching Yang. "How students react to different cyberbullying events: Past experience, judgment, perceived seriousness, helping behavior and the effect of online disinhibition." *Computers in Human Behavior* 110 (2020): 106338.

20. Suler, John. "The online disinhibition effect." *Cyberpsychology & Behavior* 7, no. 3 (2004): 321–326.

21. Patchin, Justin W., and Sameer Hinduja. "Cyberbullying among tweens in the United States: Prevalence, impact, and helping behaviors." *The Journal of Early Adolescence* 42, no. 3 (2022): 414–430.

22. Levine, Rebecca S., Amy Vatne Bintliff, and Anita Raj. "Gendered analysis of cyberbullying victimization and its associations with suicidality: Findings from the 2019 Youth Risk Behavior Survey." *Adolescents* 2, no. 2 (2022): 235–251.

23. Aboujaoude, Elias, Matthew W. Savage, Vladan Starcevic, and Wael O. Salame. "Cyberbullying: Review of an old problem gone viral." *Journal of Adolescent Health* 57, no. 1 (2015): 10–18.

24. Alhajji, Mohammed, Sarah Bass, and Ting Dai. "Cyberbullying, mental health, and violence in adolescents and associations with sex and race: Data from the 2015 youth risk behavior survey." *Global Pediatric Health* 6 (2019): 2333794X19868887.

25. Beckman, Linda, Lisa Hellström, and Laura von Kobyletzki. "Cyber bullying among children with neurodevelopmental disorders: A systematic review." *Scandinavian Journal of Psychology* 61, no. 1 (2020): 54–67.

26. Abreu, Roberto L., and Maureen C. Kenny. "Cyberbullying and LGBTQ youth: A systematic literature review and recommendations for prevention and intervention." *Journal of Child & Adolescent Trauma* 11, no. 1 (2018): 81–97.

27. Kowalski, Robin M., Gary W. Giumetti, Amber N. Schroeder, and Micah R. Lattanner. "Bullying in the digital age: A critical review and meta-analysis of cyberbullying research among youth." *Psychological Bulletin* 140, no. 4 (2014): 1073.

28. L1ght. "L1ght releases groundbreaking report on corona-related hate speech and online toxicity." *L1ght*, November 19, 2020. https://l1ght.com/l1ght-releases -groundbreaking-report-on-corona-related-hate-speech-and-online-toxicity/

29. Bacher-Hicks, Andrew, Joshua Goodman, Jennifer G. Green, and Melissa Holt. *The COVID-19 pandemic disrupted both school bullying and cyberbullying.* No. w29590. National Bureau of Economic Research, 2022.

30. Hong, Jun Sung, Jungup Lee, Dorothy L. Espelage, Simon C. Hunter, Desmond Upton Patton, and Tyrone Rivers, Jr. "Understanding the correlates of face-to-face and cyberbullying victimization among US adolescents: A social-ecological analysis." *Violence and Victims* 31, no. 4 (2016): 638–663.

31. Wade, Ann, and Tanya Beran. "Cyberbullying: The new era of bullying." *Canadian Journal of School Psychology* 26, no. 1 (2011): 44–61.

32. Williams, Kirk R., and Nancy G. Guerra. "Prevalence and predictors of internet bullying." *Journal of Adolescent Health* 41, no. 6 (2007): S14–S21.

33. Kokkinos, Constantinos M., Nafsika Antoniadou, Eleni Dalara, Anastasia Koufogazou, and Angeliki Papatziki. "Cyber-bullying, personality and coping among pre-adolescents." *International Journal of Cyber Behavior, Psychology and Learning (IJCBPL)* 3, no. 4 (2013): 55–69.

34. Tanrikulu, Ibrahim, and Marilyn Campbell. "Correlates of traditional bullying and cyberbullying perpetration among Australian students." *Children and Youth Services Review* 55 (2015): 138–146.

35. Piccoli, Valentina, Andrea Carnaghi, Michele Grassi, Marta Stragà, and Mauro Bianchi. "Cyberbullying through the lens of social influence: Predicting cyberbullying perpetration from perceived peer-norm, cyberspace regulations and ingroup processes." *Computers in Human Behavior* 102 (2020): 260–273.

36. Cross, Donna, Amy Barnes, Alana Papageorgiou, Kate Hadwen, Lydia Hearn, and Leanne Lester. "A social–ecological framework for understanding and reducing cyberbullying behaviours." *Aggression and Violent Behavior* 23 (2015): 109–117.

37. Wegge, Denis, Heidi Vandebosch, Steven Eggermont, and Sara Pabian. "Popularity through online harm: The longitudinal associations between cyberbullying and sociometric status in early adolescence." *The Journal of Early Adolescence* 36, no. 1 (2016): 86–107.

38. Bauman, Sheri, and Angela Baldasare. "Cyber aggression among college students: Demographic differences, predictors of distress, and the role of the university." *Journal of College Student Development* 56, no. 4 (2015): 317–330.

39. Guasp, A., H. Statham, V. Jadva, and I. Daly. "The School Report: The experiences of gay young people in Britain's schools in 2012. Stonewall." (2012).

40. Blais, M., J. Gervais, K. Boucher, M. Hébert, and F. Lavoie. "Prevalence of prejudice based on sexual minority status among 14 to 22-year-old youths in the province of Quebec (Canada)." *International Journal of Victimology* 11, no. 2 (2013): 1–13.

41. GLSEN, CiPHER, & CCRC. (2013). *Out online: The experiences of lesbian, gay, bisexual and transgender youth on the Internet.* GLSEN.

42. Robinson, Joseph P., and Dorothy L. Espelage. "Inequities in educational and psychological outcomes between LGBTQ and straight students in middle and high school." *Educational Researcher* 40, no. 7 (2011): 315–330.

43. Polanin, Joshua R., Dorothy L. Espelage, Jennifer K. Grotpeter, Elizabeth Spinney, Katherine M. Ingram, Alberto Valido, America El Sheikh, Cagil Torgal, and Luz Robinson. "A meta-analysis of longitudinal partial correlations between school violence and mental health, school performance, and criminal or delinquent acts." *Psychological Bulletin* 147, no. 2 (2021): 115–133.

44. European Cooperation in Science and Technology. "COST|European Cooperation in Science and Technology." *COST*, 2022. https://www.cost.eu/

45. Elsaesser, Caitlin, Beth Russell, Christine McCauley Ohannessian, and Desmond Patton. "Parenting in a digital age: A review of parents' role in preventing adolescent cyberbullying." *Aggression and Violent Behavior* 35 (2017): 62–72.

46. Brody, Nicholas, and Anita L. Vangelisti. "Bystander intervention in cyberbullying." *Communication Monographs* 83, no. 1 (2016): 94–119.

47. Torgal, Cagil, Dorothy L. Espelage, Joshua R. Polanin, Katherine M. Ingram, Luz E. Robinson, America J. El Sheikh, and Alberto Valido. "A meta-analysis of school-based cyberbullying prevention programs' impact on cyber-bystander behavior." *School Psychology Review* (2021): 1–15.

48. Zeiders, Katharine H., Lindsay T. Hoyt, and Emma K. Adam. "Associations between self-reported discrimination and diurnal cortisol rhythms among young adults: The moderating role of racial–ethnic minority status." *Psychoneuroendocrinology* 50 (2014): 280–288.

Chapter 5

Teen Sexting Is Not Child Pornography Deserving Draconian Sanction

Stop Stigmatizing Our Children

Harry Zimmerman, J.D. and Ellison Starnes

Quinn and Angel are both seventeen and have been together for sixteen months in a committed relationship. They have been intimate. Quinn and family are spending the summer across the country caring for Quinn's grandfather, who is ill. Angel misses Quinn and asks for a sexy selfie photo to have until returning home. Quinn sends a nude selfie in what some might consider to be a provocative pose (figure 5.1).

Quinn and Angel's actions make them criminals in many states across the United States. Labeled as child pornographers,[1] both might face incarceration and might be forced to register as sex offenders.[2] With any conviction, they have been stigmatized as sex offenders and saddled with criminal convictions that will affect everything from schooling to employment to housing. They are not yet eighteen years old.

The states of the United States seem to be evolving, albeit not as fast as the technology that has allowed for the increase in sexting. Fortunately, even those states that still criminalize sexting are finally recognizing that sexting between teens in an age-appropriate relationship should be treated differently. Under those circumstances, some have reduced the criminal penalty to a misdemeanor.[3] Others will allow sexting between teens as a defense to child pornography allegations. But the law, always slow to adapt to changes in society, continues to lag behind here.[4]

These latest legislative actions are consistent with statistics that point to the continuing rise in teen sexting and child development experts who acknowledge that technology and changing teen societal and dating norms mean that

Figure 5.1   Sexting between teens who may be intimate.

teen sexting is here to stay and is not necessarily unhealthy. But the law has not moved quickly enough. These experts suggest education, not criminalization, is the most effective path to address teen understanding of the potential consequences of sexting.

This chapter looks at the various state law responses to sexting through the lens of Angel and Quinn's potential consequences for sending and receiving the image and any further nonconsensual spread of that image. There is a consistent trend toward decriminalizing teen peer sexting.

But what remains is an inconsistent state patchwork of serious consequences that can destroy teenage lives before they get started. Many states still consider such an image child pornography, a felony offense, and potentially punishable with prison and sex offender registration. These laws run contrary to the opinions of more and more child development experts who eschew imprisonment and recommend harm reduction, not risk reduction methods to address the increased sexting.

With this overview of how the states of the United States treat teen sexters, you can determine how the hypothetical Angel or Quinn, or your teen might become an offender for taking a nude selfie, and in some places, victim and offender both. The consequences of teen sexting are literally an accident of location, when instead they should be a consistent matter of national public health policy to decriminalize, destigmatize, and educate minors about sexting.

THE ORIGINS OF SEXTING

Soccer superstar David Beckham's explicit text messages with an assistant allegedly inspired Canada's *The Globe and Mail* to make the first newspaper use of the term "sext messaging" in 2004. It called the practice "'the new phone sex . . . '"[5] The following year the mainstream media *Los Angeles Times'* article about "fads and trends" listed "sext-messaging."[6]

America paid little attention to sexting until a 2008 National Campaign to Prevent Teen and Unplanned Pregnancy and Cosmogirl.com survey. The survey "detailed the popularity of explicit images or texts being exchanged between teenagers. . . ." Without using the term "sext," the survey "found that roughly 1 in 5 teens had been engaged in sending naked pictures to one another."[7]

The term became part of popular culture and was used in media from the *New York Post* to the *New York Times* and from NPR to NBC. Those news stories included teens facing child pornography charges for circulating images of nude minors. One law enforcement publication picked up the baton and urged proactive enforcement of the current laws addressing sexts.[8]

"Sexting" now has a dictionary definition: "the sending of sexually explicit messages or images by cell phone."[9] It has a legal definition that considers the Internet's impact on sexting with technology allowing for wider transmission of images. Both state and federal courts have shaped sexting law.

One court was faced with a middle-school student and her friend who had circulated and sent what school authorities termed "lewd" images of themselves that had circulated among their peers off campus. The minor claimed that the term *sexting* as used in a school's policy manual was vague. But the Court disagreed, writing that "the word 'sexting' has become ubiquitous enough that it was recently added to the Merriam-Webster Dictionary."[10]

MORE AND MORE TEENS ARE SEXTING

Teen sexting is on the rise thanks to technology. There is nearly universal use of smartphones, most equipped with cameras of increasingly better quality with each new model. These cameras can shoot both still photographs and video.

Children have more access to cellphones and even receive their first cell phone at an increasingly early age. Five years ago, a Nielsen Report found that "slightly less than half (45%) of mobile kids got a service plan at 10–12 years old."[11] Text messaging was the most popular activity for children with phones (81%).[12] But the federal courts broadened the "sexting" definition, recognizing that current day laptops, computers, iPads, and tablets all have the capacity to send such messages with a Wi-Fi or cellular connection.

A 2018 study found that about one in seven (or 14.8 percent) of children between the ages of twelve and seventeen had sent sexts and about one in four (27.4 percent) had received them. A decade earlier, in a 2009 Pew Research Center study, 4 percent in that age range had sent nude or seminude images and 15 percent had received them.[13] The increase in teen sexting practice is dramatic. "It is becoming clear that a sizable number of adolescent boys and girls participate in sexting."[14] Nevertheless, the studies lament that those numbers "underestimate the percentage of teens who sext. It's not as if many people are willing to stand up and declare to everyone, 'I'm sexting and I know it.'"[15]

CHILD DEVELOPMENT EXPERTS RECOGNIZE SEXTING A PART OF TEENAGE DEVELOPMENT AND CHANGING SOCIAL NORMS

Like it or not, children are sexting—like underage alcohol drinking, sexting has become part of the coming-of-age experience for many teens. The results of a National Institute of Health study suggested "sexting may occur within the context of dating."[16] Child development experts have begun to conclude that "sexting is part of teen culture and normal adolescent sexual growth and development."[17] As another study explained, "sexting is also being recognized as a normative occurrence in the current digital era."[18]

But teen sexters face more than legal consequences. The public health consequences and the increasing prevalence of the problem eventually contributed to increased legislative activity. While research has shown that sending sexually explicit images may be connected to sexual behavior, "it is not necessarily linked to *risky* sexual behavior."[19]

Instead, research results "suggest that it might be sexually explicit words and not images that may be predictive of risky sexual behavior, which calls into question current legislation, policy, and intervention efforts focused only on nude images."

As for mental health, "links between teen sexting and mental health outcomes are more tenuous, with some researchers finding significant correlations and others reporting null effects." Studies as a whole suggest that teens who sext at a higher rate are more likely to have sex and are also more likely to have other emotional, mental health, or substance use issues. However, until sending sexually explicit images can be pinpointed as the *cause* and not simply a correlate of these negative mental health symptoms or sexual risk behaviors, it is imprudent to classify sexting as a public health risk.[20]

In Quinn and Angel's case, the emotional damage to Quinn and consequences for Angel potentially more severe if Quinn had felt coerced to send the photo—as some teens do. "Research shows that sexting can be an online extension to offline sexual coercion in adolescent relationships and that those who experienced sexting coercion endorsed more symptoms of anxiety, depression, and generalized trauma."[21] Similarly, as will be discussed later in this chapter, their breakup might have led an angry Angel to post the image to friends or online without Quinn's consent in the heat of the moment.

Quinn could face potential harassment, cyberbullying, or blackmail. Mental health consequences from these behaviors "can lead to depression and even thoughts of suicide among those who have been victimized. Further, once a sext is sent, the sender has no control of what happens to the picture and even if it is sent via apps that claim to delete the pictures, there are still digital footprints and screenshots can be taken."[22] In addition to any mental health consequences Quinn might suffer, Angel's distribution of the image would likely lead to more serious criminal penalties.

Legal consequences are often calibrated based on the victim's nonlegal consequences. But those who have studied nonlegal consequences acknowledge there is still insufficient research on teen sexting nonlegal consequences. Even the meta-analysis of twenty-three studies with 41,723 participants, while generally finding of a correlation "between sexual behavior and mental health risk factors in youth," concludes with a recommendation for further research to "discern the mechanisms behind sexting and its association with potential risk factors."

The same meta-analysis produced enough information showing a "shift in perspective . . . mirrored in US, European, and Canadian laws surrounding sexting, which recognize instances in which sexting can be both harmful and harmless." The same study urged prioritizing education "to ensure that adolescents and youth are equipped with the tools they need to navigate their personal and social development in a technological world."[23]

Consequently, while the full extent of the effects of teen sexting has yet to be determined, experts have reached three significant conclusions: technology and teen exposure to more and more sexual content through the media make further growth of sexting inevitable; sexting has become part of a teen's normal sexual development and social norms; and a noncriminalized, harm reduction approach is the best way to address teen sexting.[24]

HOW SEXTING BECAME CHILD PORNOGRAPHY

U.S. Supreme Court Justice Potter Stewart, discussing the term "hard-core pornography," famously wrote: "I shall not today attempt further to define the kinds of material I understand to be embraced within that shorthand description; and perhaps I could never succeed in intelligibly doing so. But I know it when I see it."[25] If Supreme Court justices are stymied in defining pornography, defining child pornography in the digital age has created even greater difficulty. Leaving that definition to Congress and state legislatures has only created a patchwork of law leading to uncertainty about where teen sexting fits into the mix.[26]

The U.S. Supreme Court has found that Congress' primary purpose for enacting the federal child pornography statute was to prevent the "use of children as subjects of pornographic materials [which is] harmful to psychological, emotional, and mental health of the child."[27] It has often found a permanent recording of a child's image cause of psychological trauma to the child.[28] Analyzing a state pornography law, the High Court in endorsed the idea of "severe criminal penalties" like lengthy prison terms, mandatory minimum sentences, and sex offender registration as a means for drying up the child pornography market.[29]

Teen sexting generally does not justify these draconian criminal penalties. Only when images are produced through express or implied coercion, or when images are distributed more widely without the consent of the individual portrayed, does it cause the potential for psychological trauma that the Supreme Court found most troubling. Consequently, criminal penalties for sexting will lead to additional trauma for the child.

One commentator has noted: "The harm the child suffers from the draconian penalties for violating child pornography statues parallels the psychological, emotional, or mental, harm already suffered by the child from the knowledge that the image may be publicly disseminated."[30] Prosecution results in the minor being labeled as a sex offender with a criminal record and its concomitant damage to educational and career opportunities.

Many academic commentators have observed that child pornography laws were intended for adult offenders and not for teens. "Since these laws were meant to target intergenerational sex crimes, it makes little sense to read into them the criminalization of consensual peer-to-peer activities." Those laws were designed to prevent exploitation of minors through the production of child pornography. "Because there is no child abuse, repeated victimization, or predation, consensual teen sexting should not be classified as child pornography, especially in cases lacking malicious or wrongful intent to harm the individual depicted in the image."[31]

Given the rise in teen sexting, serious criminal penalties for child pornography have failed to act as an effective deterrent. Most teens would be surprised to know that sexting could lead to criminal prosecution. The penalties for teen sexting under child pornography laws, with the potential to ruin the minor's life, are not warranted for youthful indiscretions without further distribution or coercion in production.

Teen sexting prosecutions do not serve the purposes of such statutes that are "aimed at constraining pedophilic desires, capturing of the adults who take advantage of children, and eliminating the market for child pornography."[32] Nevertheless, the gray areas contained in the language of state child pornography laws, where states have not legislated different penalties for specific teen sexting behavior or as a defense to child pornography prosecutions, continue to endanger minors who are just exploring their sexuality as part of the today's teenage social and dating arena.

THE STATE LEGISLATIVE RESPONSE TO SEXTING

Thomas Jefferson said:

> I am not an advocate for frequent changes in laws and constitutions, but laws and institutions must go hand in hand with the progress of the human mind. As that becomes more developed, more enlightened, as new discoveries are made, new truths discovered and manners and opinions change, with the change of circumstances, institutions must advance also to keep pace with the times. We might as well require a man to wear still the coat which fitted him when a boy as civilized society to remain ever under the regimen of their barbarous ancestors.

Although the criminalization of teen sexting has been criticized by academic writers for the last twenty years, it is only within the last decade that states have moved with some alacrity to address the issue. State action has apparently been motivated not so much by that criticism, but rather by "the media's response to teenage sexuality."[33] Perhaps, state legislators also had nightmares of their teenage children prosecuted and incarcerated as criminals with sex offender registration for their sexting.

However, there are certain states that Jefferson might find not to have tread that more enlightened path of change. For example, Wisconsin's law prohibiting sexual exploitation of a child includes sexting images of minors under eighteen. The age of the creator and the sender makes no difference. Sexual activity is not required. Only a more subjective "lewd exhibit of intimate parts" is required.

In the case of Quinn's sexy selfie, the creation and sending of the photograph makes Quinn guilty of sexual exploitation for creating the photo and further culpability for distributing it to Angel. In Wisconsin, Quinn could face a decade or more in prison. If Angel had passed the photo further, regardless of intent, Angel could face a similar penalty.[34]

Fortunately, states are moving away from such draconian penalties for teen sexting behavior. State law seems to now follow two general trends. First, several western states have enacted complex sexting statutes which vary punishment based on several factors that distinguish punishment for a recipient, possessor, or distributor. The legislation is complex due to the various factors that can alter the punishment a sexting minor receives.

These statutes all were enacted after 2016. Each applies to minors under the age of eighteen and to both the sender and recipient of sexts. Each increases the punishment for malicious distribution of the image. Other factors affecting punishment include any use of coercion or the defendant's status as a repeat offender.

Colorado's statute creates three tiers of punishment: consenting sexters who are in the same general age face a civil infraction, a recipient who redistributes a sext commits a misdemeanor, and coercion or the defendant's repeat offender status may lead to a more serious sentence. Wyoming and Idaho also provide three tiers of punishment for the more typical instance of sexting between two consenting teens.[35] The statutes generally do not apply if the nonconsenting recipient of a sext reports it to someone in a position of authority or deletes it.[36]

Most of these comprehensive state sexting statutes have reduced the punishment for sexting to a misdemeanor offense and allowed for an affirmative defense when the recipient of a sext notifies a person in a position of authority.[37] But an affirmative defense still requires the minor to prove certain factors to avoid prosecution or punishment.

States appear to be moving toward these comprehensive statutes covering all aspects of sexting, including the production, distribution, and possession of sexts. Before 2011, only North Dakota had such a comprehensive statute.[38] Six out of the eight state sexting statutes enacted since 2011 have been comprehensive.[39] Angel and Quinn would face a much better potential outcome in these states. But even a misdemeanor conviction is still a criminal conviction.

The second trend in America has seen states across the country amending their child pornography statutes to exempt or reduce the penalties potentially applicable to sexting teens.[40] Yet those laws continue to define sexting as child pornography, whether occurring between minors or a minor and an adult. A minority of state statutes limit these lesser penalties or exempted status to media depicting nudity and not sexually explicit content.[41]

Increasingly, state laws have begun to exempt minors from these child pornography statutes, even those depicting sexually explicit conduct, or have reduced the penalties minors face for violating the law. But most states still lack these "Romeo and Juliet" laws that make prosecution or penalty dependent on age.[42] Previously, even those states that had altered their child pornography statutes to create an exemption for minors had made it an affirmative defense instead of a blanket exemption or penalty reduction, placing the burden on the minor to show the child pornography law did not apply.[43]

Generally, states that have chosen to implement exemptions or penalty reductions require that the depicted minor be at least fourteen years of age, have given permission for the image or produced it themselves, and the recipient was younger than eighteen years old.[44]

Whether a state has carved out a child pornography exemption, created an affirmative defense, or reduced its punishment for sexting, all have relied on similar factors in mitigation or aggravation. Those considerations have included the youth of the sender, lack of image solicitation, the image being immediately destroyed on receipt, or the minor notifying an adult authority figure after receiving the image. These states all have recognized, to one degree or another, that teen sexting should not necessarily lead to felony conviction, sex offender registration, and a destroyed future before that teen has reached the age of eighteen.

What does that mean for Angel and Quinn? As the laws differ from state to state, it is an accident of location that determines how their sexting would be treated. A more progressive state like Colorado might impose a small fine for a civil infraction, if they are pursued at all for the indiscretion. If they merely share the image between them, and it travels no further, it might never come to light. But the extended hypothetical posed here has the young couple breaking up, no surprise given their age, and Angel sharing the image with friends or posting it online.

The latest statutory changes have generally meant that states do not punish possession of a sext. Punishment would follow if the recipient of a sext distributes or threatens to distribute the sext to coerce, intimidate, or embarrass the sender of the sext. Even then, Wyoming only increases its sexting punishment to its most serious misdemeanor.[45]

But posting images online can prove to be a punishment difference maker because it can be deemed revenge porn. This act is generally defined as distributing a sexually graphic image without the consent of the person depicted in the context of an intimate relationship.[46] As of the end of 2021, there were forty-eight states with revenge porn statutes. They vary widely in the elements needed for conviction, definitions, exceptions, and penalties.[47]

These newer statutes remain a part of a larger divide about whether the sexting statute applies to sexts depicting only nudity or sexts depicting explicit sexual conduct. While Wyoming's statute is relatively lenient to teen sexters, punishing it as a status offense, the statute only applies to nude images or videos. In Wyoming, further dissemination or even capturing the image without the knowledge of the individual depicted can nevertheless lead to jail. As can more explicit images. On the other hand, Idaho's least severe punishment for sexting is a misdemeanor, but it applies to sexts depicting both nudity and explicit sexual conduct.[48]

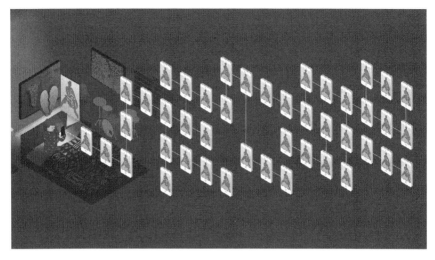

Figure 5.2   Widespread nonconsensual distribution of sexts as a potential sexting consequence.

THE COURT DECISIONS HAVE NOT HELPED TO CLARIFY STATUTES THAT DO NOT DISTINGUISH SEXTING FROM CHILD PORNOGRAPHY

Those states without specific statutes addressing sexting have left it to their courts to decide if teen sexting is child pornography and then has any consequences. Courts have punished child pornography and sexting similarly and have considered them equally violative of the child pornography law. By failing to acknowledge technological and social change, Jefferson might say courts are still wearing their childhood coats. Statutes have not been specific enough to address sexting issues. Courts have not distinguished between teen sexters and predators or criminal spreaders of images on the Internet that the statutes are intended to address (figure 5.2).

Maryland has yet to add sexting to its statute, and its courts have continued to label teen sexting, even when not considered obscene, as child pornography under its state law. "The General Assembly has not updated the statute's language since the advent of sexting and thus we may not read into the statute an exception for minors."[49] Consequently, the Maryland law made the minor there both a victim and offender of the child pornography law, even as the Court acknowledged that the sexual conduct depicted was not criminal.[50]

Oregon is another state that does not distinguish between teen sexting and child pornography.[51] No Oregon law shields teens from criminal prosecution for sexting under a variety of invasion of privacy and exploitation of a minor charges. An Oregon conviction may still require the teen to register as a sex offender. Worst yet, as no one else need be involved in creating the image, nude selfies may be prosecutable as child pornography. Like Maryland, teens that capture their own images are considered sexually exploited victims and criminal offenders.

In Oregon, the courts have had to step in to mitigate some particularly harsh sentences for teen sexting. One defendant's mandatory minimum twenty-five-year sentence was overturned and the case sent back for resentencing. The defendant there was between the ages of sixteen and eighteen years old when he "persuaded several girls who were between two to four years younger to take and send to him by cell phone nude self-portraits." The Court found the sentence unconstitutionally disproportionate.[52]

TOWARD A HARM REDUCTION AND NOT A RISK REDUCTION POLICY

Risk reduction seeks to eliminate the pitfalls our youth might be exposed to—"a worldview that reflects the notion that we need to save kids from themselves and from a host of potential evils that surround them. The problem with this mentality, though, is that it promotes moral panic and fear mongering, as well as rule-based restrictive and punitive controls on their life."[53]

In harm reduction, as explained by professors Patchin and Hinduja, we assume "some youth are going to engage in certain risky behaviors, and with that in mind informs policies and practices designed to reduce the negatives that may occur." Those researchers analogize sexting to teens who use alcohol or other drugs. In risk reduction, there is a focus on criminal penalties; harm reduction looks to avoid the worst possible consequences through counseling and guidance. For teen drinkers, it might be as simple as "give someone your car keys before you start drinking and have a designated driver, or to sleep it off where you are."[54]

With the recognition that some minors will still experiment, the need to educate their less-than fully developed, risk-taking brains through harm reduction should more than outweigh any need to punish them. "Education not only involves describing dangers and attempting to deter immature and unwise choices, but also how to make sure the backlash from those choices is not fatal."[55] It is the same principle that inspires clean needle programs and diversion programs, in lieu of incarceration, for those addicted to alcohol or illegal narcotics.

Professors Patchin and Hinduja have written about the need for a safe sexting curriculum, "to teach youth about the consequences of participation, and how to mitigate those." They recognize that such an idea would be an "evolution of sex education in the United States." Nevertheless, as they explain, "these might be provocative ideas here in the U.S., but they are not new when looking elsewhere in the world."[56]

CONCLUSION

The "thought of educating kids about safe sexting may make you cringe." But two generations ago, "the same emotional reaction happened back when safe sex education was first introduced."[57]

Sexting among teens is not going away and technology and social networks will continue to make it easier to do and more widespread. Parents should be active on two fronts: first, calm down; talk to your children about sexting at an early age and use realistic scenarios like Angel and Quinn to explain the consequences and how to keep themselves safe. Use someone in the news with similar issues so it does not become about your child. If your relationship is difficult or you don't feel comfortable discussing sexting, have someone else speak with your child.

Most importantly, any images that might have been nonconsensual or distributed more widely need to be preserved for law enforcement. Otherwise, your child should understand why any questionable images should be deleted immediately.[58] If your child is sexting, professors Patchin and Hinduja provide ten practical tips for your teen to guard against further distribution. They include not sharing any images received with anyone, never including a face or other identifying marks like tattoos in an image, turning off the device location services for social media apps, and using apps that automatically delete images.[59]

The second step parents should take is to determine what the law says about teens who sext in your state. If your legislature has held to a sexting as child pornography philosophy, use citizen action to help them abandon their childhood coats and create an amended statute that reflects changes in technology and society.

Professor Amy Adler of NYU Law School, who has written extensively about sexting, summed it up best more than a decade ago: "Child pornography law was crafted to protect children from pedophiles, that's the idea behind it," said Adler. "But now what we have is the law applying to situations where the child himself or herself is making the pornography. So it's this odd situation where suddenly the pornographer and the victim are one and the same person. And in my view that's not the kind of scenario that child pornography law should cover."[60]

While many state legislatures have adapted their laws to fit a teen sexting scenario, half of them have not clearly distinguished sexting from child pornography and continue to impose drastic criminal sanctions. The time has come for America to deal with sexting in a more uniform and progressive way. Teens who sext should not be scarred for life from the very laws that are designed to protect them.

NOTES

1. In 2014, a seventeen-year-old boy faced felony charges of "manufacturing and distributing child pornography" in Virginia for "Sending a video text of his adolescent junk to his girlfriend." The *Washington Post* reported he "may end up behind bars until he's 21, and could be on the state sex offender database for the rest of his life." Jeffrey Van Camp, "Underage sexting isn't ruining lives, draconian laws are (and we need to change them)," *Digital Trends*, July 12, 2014, https://www.digitaltrends.com /mobile/underage-sexting-isnt-ruining-lives/.

2. Jorge Canal is on the sex offenders registry in Iowa. At eighteen, "he was convicted of distributing obscene materials to a minor after he sent a picture of his penis by cellphone to a 14-year-old female friend who had requested it." Tamar Lewin, "Rethinking Sex Offender Law for Youth Texting," *New York Times*, March 20, 2010, https://www.nytimes.com/2010/03/21/us/21sexting.html?ref=technology.

3. In Georgia, sexting is a misdemeanor if:

- the child in the image is at least fourteen.
- the image was created with the child's permission.
- the defendant possessed the image with the child's permission.
- the defendant was eighteen or younger.
- the defendant did not distribute the image further or the image was not distributed for either a commercial purpose or to harass, intimidate, or embarrass the child in the image.

Ga. Code Ann. § 16-12-100.2(c)(3) (West 2019).

Nebraska's law now allows for a defense to child pornography charges under two separate circumstances, based on the ages of the sexting participants. Defendants under nineteen may raise the defense if

- the image of sexually explicit conduct shows a child over fifteen.
- the image was knowing and voluntarily produced by child depicted.
- the image was knowingly and voluntarily provided by the child depicted.
- the image is of only one child.
- the defendant has not transmitted the image to anyone else except for the child in the image who sent it.
- the child was not coerced into creating or sending the image.

Defendants under eighteen may raise the defense when

- the age difference between the defendant and the child in the image is less than four years.
- the child in the image knowingly and voluntarily produced it.

- there is only one child in the image.
- the defendant has only transmitted the image to the child who produced it and not any further.
- the defendant did not coerce the child to create or send the image.

Neb. Rev. Stat. Ann § 28-813.01 (West 2022).

4. For a comprehensive chart of state-by-state sexting laws, see the 2022-dated sexting laws chart from the Cyberbullying Research Center found at https://cyberbullying.org/sexting-laws.

5. Eli Rosenberg, "In Weiner's Wake, a Brief History of the Word 'Sexting,'" The Atlantic, June 9, 2011, https://www.theatlantic.com/national/archive/2011/06/brief-history-sexting/351598/.

6. Rosenberg, "Brief History."

7. Rosenberg, "Brief History."

8. Rosenberg, "Brief History."

9. https://www.merriam-webster.com/dictionary/sexting. Ironically, one of the dictionary's examples of the use of the word in a sentence goes to the heart of this chapter: "Researchers have largely advocated for the decriminalization of consensual*sexting*."

10. *S. N. B. v. Pearland Indep. Sch. Dist.*, 120 F. Supp. 3d 620, 627 (S.D. Tex. 2014)(fn 6. omitted). Sexting is "'the practice of sending or posting sexually suggestive text messages and images, including nude or semi-nude photographs, via cellular telephones or over the Internet.'" (*Id.*, citing *Miller v. Mitchell*, 598 F.3d 139, 143 (3d Cir. 2010)), https://www.courtlistener.com/opinion/https://www.courtlistener.com/opinion/259/miller-v-mitchell/?page=2.

Legal dictionaries also include the word "sexting," citing and origin date of 2005 and defining it as "the creation, possession, or distribution of sexually explicit images via cellphones. The term is a portmanteau of sex and texting." *In re S.K.*, 466 Md. 31, 215 A.3d 300 (2019) (citing Black's Law Dictionary, 11th Edition, 2019).

11. Nielsen Report, "Mobile Kids: The Parent, the Child and the Smartphone," February 28, 2017, https://www.nielsen.com/us/en/insights/article/2017/mobile-kids--the-parent-the-child-and-the-smartphone/.

12. Nielsen Report, "Mobile Kids."

13. Sheri Madigan, Anh Ly, Christina L. Rash, Joris Van Ouytsel, and Jeff R. Temple, Prevalence of Multiple Forms of Sexting Behavior Among Youth A Systematic Review and Meta-analysis, JAMA Pediatrics, April, 2018, 328, https://jamanetwork.com/journals/jamapediatrics/fullarticle/2673719.

14. Madigan et al., "Prevalence of Sexting Behavior," 328.

15. Bruce Y. Lee, Here Is How Much Sexting Among Teens Has Increased, Forbes, September 8, 2018, https://www.forbes.com/sites/brucelee/2018/09/08/here-is-how-much-sexting-among-teens-has-increased/?sh=47509ed436f1.

16. Jeff R. Temple, Ph.D., Jonathan A. Paul, Ph.D., Patricia van den Berg, Ph.D., Vi Donna.

Le, B.S., Amy McElhany, B.A., and Brian W. Temple, M.D., "Teen sexting and its association with sexual behaviors," Arch Pediatr Adolesc Med., September, 2012, 5, https://www.ncbi.nlm.nih.gov/pmc/articles/PMC3626288/.

17. Dawn Marie Murphy and Becky Spencer, "Teens Experience With Sexting: A Grounded Study" ("Discussion"), *Journal of Pediatric Health Care*, July 1, 2021, https://www.jpedhc.org/article/S0891-5245(20)30311-4/fulltext.

18. Camille Mori, Jeff R. Temple, Dillon Browne, Sheri Madigan, "Association of Sexting With Sexual Behaviors and Mental Health Among Adolescents A Systematic Review and Meta-Analysis," *JAMA Pediatrics*, June 7, 2019, 777, fns. 75, 76 omitted, https://jamanetwork.com/journals/jamapediatrics/fullarticle/2735639.

19. Kimberly O'Connor, Michelle Drouin, Nicholas Yergens, & Genni Newsham, "Sexting Legislation in the United States and Abroad: A Call for Uniformity," International Journal of Cyber Criminology, 2017, Vol. 11(2): 218, 222, emphasis by authors, http://cybercrimejournal.com/O%27Connoretalvol11issue2IJCC2017.pdf.

20. O'Connor, et al., "Sexting Legislation," 222–223.

21. Elizabeth J. Jeglic, "Teen Sexting: Guidelines for Parents," *Psychology Today*, (January 11, 2020), https://www.psychologytoday.com/us/blog/protecting-children -sexual-abuse/202001/teen-sexting-guidelines-parents.

22. Jeglic, "Teen Sexting," *Psychology Today*.

23. Mori et al., "Association of Sexting with Sexual Behaviors," 777.

24. Mori et al., "Association of Sexting with Sexual Behaviors," 777.

25. *Jacobellis v. Ohio*, 378 U.S. 184 (1964).

26. Federal prosecution of juveniles for sexting is not a likely occurrence. The Federal Juvenile Delinquency Act generally provides that, where possible, juveniles should be prosecuted in state courts. 18 U.S.C. §§ 1466A, 2251, 2252, 2252A, 5032 (2020), https://www.law.cornell.edu/uscode/text/18/1466A.

27. *New York v. Ferber*, 458 U.S. 747, 758 (1982), https://advance.lexis.com/ document?crid=bbff81cf-8f36-4cea-9936-3fffed3a6a5e&pddocfullpath=%2Fshared %2Fdocument%2Fcases%2Furn%3AcontentItem%3A3S4X-5D70-003B-S4C7 -00000-00&pdsourcegroupingtype=&pdcontentcomponentid=6443&pdmfid =1000516&pdisurlapi=true.

28. *Ferber* at 759.

29. *Ferber* at 760.

30. Jessica Sabbah-Mani, *Note, Sexting Education: An Educational Approach to Solving the Media Fueled Sexting Dilemma*, Spring, 2015 24 S. Cal. Interdis. L.J. 529, 543.

31. Sabbah-Mani, *Sexting Education*, 544.

32. Sabbah-Mani, *Sexting Education*, 560.

33. Blaire Bayliss, Comment, *The Kids Are Alright: Teen Sexting, Child Pornography Charges, and the Criminalization of Adolescent Sexuality*, 91 Colo. L. Rev. 252, 262 (2020).

34. Wis. Stat. §§ 939.50, 939.617, 948.01, 948.05 (2020).

35. Colo. Rev. Stat. § 18-7-109 (2021) (enacted in 2017). Civil infractions in Colorado are punishable by up to a $50 fine "or participation in a program addressing the risks and consequences of such behavior." *People ex rel. T.B.*, 2019 CO 53, ¶ 3, 445 P.3d 1049, 1051; Colo. Rev. Stat. § 18-7-109(3). In Wyoming, see Wyo. Stat. § 6-4-305 (202) (enacted in 2017); and for Idaho see Idaho Code § 18-1507a (2021) (enacted in 2016). Nevertheless, even a misdemeanor conviction can lead to extended

incarceration. While misdemeanors are broken down in some states into several types, a misdemeanor is "typically a crime punishable by less than 12 months in jail." Cornell Law School, Legal Information Institute, https://www.law.cornell.edu/wex/misdemeanor.

36. In Idaho, the statute excludes minors who received sexts if they distributed "the image to a part, guardian . . . or a law enforcement official for the purpose of reporting the activity." *See* Idaho Code § 18-1507a(6); or see Wyo. Stat. § 6-4-305(b)(ii), which excludes possessors who "inadvertently came into possession of the image and took reasonable steps to destroy the image or notify a person in a position of authority of its existence"; or, Colo. Rev. Stat. § 18-7-109(2)(a), which excludes minors from a possession of child pornography charge if they "took reasonable steps to either destroy or delete the image within seventy-two hours after initially viewing" it.

37. Colo. Rev. Stat. § 18-7-109 (2021); S.D. Codified Laws § 26-10-33 (2021).

38. N.D. Cent. Code. § 12.1-27.1-01 (2021).

39. *Compare* Wyo. Stat. § 6-4-305 (2021); S.D. Codified Laws § 26-10-33 (2021); Colo. Rev. Stat. § 18-7-109 (2021); Idaho Code § 18-1507a (2021); 18 Pa. Cons. Stat. § 6312 (2021); W. Va. Code § 49-4-717 (2021); *with* Fla. Stat. § 847.0141 (2021), and Kan. Stat. § 21-5610 (2021).

40. *See* Ark. Code Ann. § 5-27-609 (2021) (enacted in 2016, reducing penality under child exploitation statute); and Me. Stat. 17-A § 284 (2021) and N.M. Stat. § 30-6A-3 (2021). The latter two statutes were enacted in 2016 and exempt sexting teens from the child exploitation statute.

41. *See, e.g.,* Wyo. Stat. §. 6-4-305; Fla. Stat. § 847.0141.

42. In Maine, there is no violation of the law "if the person depicted is 14 or 15 years of age and the person is less than 5 years older than the person depicted." Me. Stat. 17-A § 284 (2021) (enacted in 2016). New Mexico is similar. N.M. Stat. § 30-6A-3 (2021) (enacted in 2016). In Kansas, those under nineteen may possess photos of minors sixteen or older. Kan. Stat. § 21-5610 (2022) (enacted in 2016).

43. *See* Ariz. Rev. Stat. Ann. § 8-309 (2021) and Utah Code Ann. § 76-10-1206 (2021), each creating an affirmative defense.

44. *See* Me. Stat. 17-A § 284(1) (enacted in 2016); N.M. Stat. § 30-6A-3(b); Ga. Code § 16-12-100(3)(a).

45. There is a potential misdemeanor punishment of up to six months in a juvenile detention facility "if, with the intent to coerce, intimidate, torment, harass or otherwise cause emotional distress to another minor, the minor disseminates or threatens to disseminate a nude image." Wyo. Stat. §. 6-4-305(d), (f)(2).

46. Danielle Keats Citron & Mary Anne Franks, *Criminalizing Revenge Porn*, 49 Wake Forest L. Rev. 345, 346 (2014), https://scholarship.law.bu.edu/cgi/viewcontent.cgi?article=1643&context=faculty_scholarship

47. Christian Nisttáhuz, Comment: *Fifty States of Gray: A Comparative Analysis of "Revenge-Porn" Legislation Throughout the United States and Texas' Relationship Privacy Act*, 50 Tex. Tech L. Rev. 333, 357 (2018), COMMENT: FIFTY STATES OF GRAY: A COMPARATIVE ANALYSIS OF "REVENGE-PORN" LEGISLATION THROUGHOUT THE UNITED STATES AND TEXAS'S RELATIONSHIP PRIVACY ACT: Comment , 50 Tex. Tech L. Rev. 333.

48. "'Status offense'" means an offense which, if committed by an adult, would not constitute an act punishable as a criminal offense by the laws of this state or a violation of a municipal ordinance."Wyo. Stat. Ann. §§ 7-1-107, 6-4-305(a)(iv) (2021);Idaho Code § 18-1507a(1) (2021).

49. *In re S.K.*, 466 Md. 31, 36, 215 A.3d 300, 303 (2019)

50. *In re S.K.*, 466 Md. 31, 42, 54, 215 A.3d 300, 306, 314 (2019). In contrast, in Canada, the Supreme Court of Canada has carved out an exception under its child pornography law for those under eighteen who privately sext, even if it portrays the minor engaging in a sex act. See Lara Karaian and Dillon Brady, "Revisiting the 'Private Use Exception' to Canada's Child Pornography Laws: Teenage Sexting, Sex-Positivity, Pleasure, and Control in the Digital Age," 56 *Osgoode Hall Law Journal* 301, 302 (May 21, 2020) ARTICLE: Revisiting the "Private Use Exception" to Canada's Child Pornography Laws: Teenage Sexting, Sex-Positivity, Pleasure, and Control in the Digital Age, 56 Osgoode Hall L.J. 301 ("In R v Sharpe, the Supreme Court of Canada read in a 'private use exception' to the offence of possessing child pornography. The Court reasoned that youths' self-created expressive material and private recordings of lawful sexual activity—created by or depicting the accused and held by the accused exclusively for private use—would pose little or no risk to children and may in fact be of significance to adolescent self-fulfillment, self-actualization, sexual exploration, and identity.)

51. ORS § 163.670.

52. *State v. Carey Martin*, 293 Ore. App. 611, 643, 480 P.3d 98, 118.

53. Justin W. Patchin and Sameer Hinduja, "It's Time to Teach Safe Sexting" 66 Journal of Adolescent Health 140-143 (2020), cited online by Cyberbullying Research Center https://cyberbullying.org/it-is-time-to-teach-safe-sexting.

54. Patchin and Hinduja, "It's Time to Teach Safe Sexting."

55. Patchin and Hinduja, "It's Time to Teach Safe Sexting."

56. Patchin and Hinduja, "It's Time to Teach Safe Sexting."

57. Patchin and Hinduja, "It's Time to Teach Safe Sexting."

58. Julie Jargon, Sexting Among Kids Is Bigger Than Ever—and Often Illegal. Here's How to Talk to Your Child (montefiore.org), (June 5, 2021), https://www.montefiore.org/body.cfm?id=3132&action=detail&ref=1983&iirf_redirect=1

59. Patchin and Hinduja, "It's Time to Teach Safe Sexting."

60. "On Nightline, Amy Adler discusses legal consequences of sexting," NYU Law News, April 2, 2010, https://www.law.nyu.edu/news/ADLER_NIGHTLINE_SEXTING

Chapter 6

Why Do People Believe in Conspiracy Theories?—The Role of the Media

Victor C. Strasburger

This is truly the golden era of conspiracy theories.
>—Trevor Noah, 2022 at the White
House Correspondents' Dinner

I'm not into conspiracy theories, except the ones that are true or involve dentists.
>—Filmmaker Michael Moore
(quoted in Olmsted, 2019, p. 11)

"Why look for conspiracy when stupidity can explain so much."
>—Johann Wolfgang von Goethe (The
Sorrows of Young Werther, May 4, 1771)

"All conspiracy theories are the product of the subconscious attempt of an ignorant yet creative mind to counteract the fear of the unknown with tales of fantasy."
>—Abhijit Naskar, Mucize Insan:
When The World is Family

"Something died in the American people on November 22, 1963—call it idealism, innocence or the quest for moral excellence. It is the transformation of human beings which is the authentic reason and motive for the Kennedy murder."
>—James Shelby Downard, King-Kill/33

"Jack Ruby's assassination of Lee Harvey Oswald was the 1963 equivalent of the second plane hitting the Twin Towers on 9/11—

it turned a seemingly random act of violence into an orchestrated conspiracy, imagined in Ruby's case."

—Stewart Stafford (https://bukrate
.com/author/stewart-stafford)

A global Confederacy of Dunces is being established, whose cretinous values are transmitted by bizarre memes that crisscross the Internet at a dizzying speed, and which are always accepted uncritically as the finest nuggets of truth. Woe betide anyone who challenges the Confederacy. They will be immediately trolled.

—Joe Dixon, Dumbocalypse Now:
The First Dunning-Kruger President

"You're only a nut if you're wrong."

—Angela Mullins, Working for Uncle Henry

Why do people believe in conspiracy theories? This has become one of the most crucial and concerning issues of our time. After all, the most common conspiracy theory currently circulating—that Donald Trump won the 2020 Presidential election—has virtually torn the country apart, led to the January 6th Capitol insurrection, and imperiled nearly 250 years of American democracy. As two political experts observed, "A world in which substantial numbers of Americans believe that the duly elected president of the United States is not legitimate is a world in which political compromise becomes substantially more difficult (Mann & Orenstein, 2016)."

Figure 6.0   Copyright © Cartoon Bank. Used with permission.

What could be more important than understanding why people believe in conspiracy theories and what role the media play? We now find ourselves living in what one group of authors calls "The Age of Misinformation" (Bessi et al., 2015).

An FBI report (Grant, 2019) cites conspiracy theories as "a new domestic terror threat." Per the report, "The FBI assesses these conspiracy theories very likely will emerge, spread, and evolve in the modern information marketplace, occasionally driving both groups and individual extremists to carry out criminal or violent acts."

Some adults may be able to distinguish "fake news" from the genuine article, but children and teenagers are much less intellectually and experientially competent. Believing in "fake news" and conspiracy theories has led— and can lead—to disastrous consequences for individuals and for society as a whole. One not-so-trivial example: As the AIDS denialists gained more attention, political leaders like former South African president Thabo Mbeki delayed the deployment of antiretroviral drugs, resulting in the deaths of an estimated 330,000 people between 2000 and 2005 (Chigwedere et al., 2008). Therefore, it is crucial to understand why people seem to be believing in them in ever greater numbers (Jimenez, 2019).

WHAT IS A CONSPIRACY THEORY?

The Oxford English Dictionary defines conspiracy theory as "the theory that an event or phenomenon occurs as a result of a conspiracy between interested parties; spec. a *belief* that some covert but influential agency (typically political in motivation and oppressive in intent) is responsible for an unexplained event." Importantly, the term refers to a *hypothesized*—as opposed to a proven—conspiracy.

Definitions of what is a conspiracy theory may differ, but one thing is certain—such theories do not necessarily need to be wrong or inaccurate. Labeling something as a conspiracy theory does not automatically make it outlandish or untrue, although the term is used most often by people to describe a clandestine plot by powerful conspirators and/or the government that seems totally wacky—for example, Steven Jones' allegation that the horrendous slaughter of twenty-six people at Sandy Hook Elementary School including twenty young children by Adam Lanza was a "false flag"* operation, "completely fake" and a "giant hoax" perpetrated by opponents of the Second Amendment. He was subsequently found guilty of defamation in

---

* "False flag" refers to the pirate strategy of flying a friendly flag instead of their own Jolly Roger in order to attract and pillage ships.

two lawsuits (https://www.cbsnews.com/news/alex-jones-bankruptcy-filing
-infowars-defamation-suits-sandy-hook/). Or there is the QAnon contention
that a global cabal of Satan-worshipping, cannibalistic child sex traffickers
exists in Washington, DC, whose members include Hilary Clinton, Tom
Hanks, and Oprah Winfrey (Wagner, 2021).

True conspiracies do exist: the plot(s) to assassinate Abraham Lincoln,
the Tuskegee syphilis experiments, Iran Contragate, Watergate, weapons of
mass destruction in Iraq. One of the most fascinating true, well documented,
and relatively unknown examples is Operation Northwoods. In March 1962,
the Joint Chiefs of Staff proposed a plan to Secretary of Defense Robert
McNamara to entice Americans into supporting an invasion of Castro's Cuba.
The proposal involved having the U.S. military explode bombs in U.S cities,
sink boats containing Cuban refugees attempting to enter the United States,
and assassinate Cuban dissidents in the United States; therefore, trying to
frame Castro as the instigator. They apparently went so far as to contemplate
blowing up John Glenn's first suborbital space flight. Fortunately, President
Kennedy nixed the plan (Olmstead, 2019).

In the current political climate, odds are that conspiracy theories will be
false. As the OED mentions, many conspiracy theories point to government
involvement and cover-ups and involve murder (e.g., the Kennedy assassination, Martin Luther King's assassination, Marilyn Monroe's death). But to
automatically dismiss such theories is unhelpful and—as recently seen with
the January 6th insurrection at the Capitol—politically and sometimes even
physically dangerous. In addition, such theories are not solely promulgated
by the conservative right.

In the world of conspiracy theories, nothing is as it seems—but "the truth
is out there" (per the *X*-Files). There are conspirators who are powerful, they
have been able to escape detection, the truth rests on some scrap of obscure and
overlooked piece of information, and ultimately the conspiracy is impossible to
disprove (Brotherton, 2016). In fact, a 2019 report from the FBI labels conspiracy theories as "a new domestic terror threat" (Table 6.1) (Monmouth, 2022).

While it is severely tempting to want to set the poor foolhardy folks
straight, it is likewise impossible to actually be able to do so, even with "the
facts." They hold their beliefs with almost religious fervor. For example, after

Table 6.1   Why Conspiracy Theories May Be Dangerous

- Unhealthy, potentially dangerous manipulation of public opinion
- Increasing the risk of extremist or violent behavior
- Putting fringe, debunked, or false ideas into mainstream circulation
- Interfering with important public health initiatives
- Undermining confidence in public leaders and institutions
- Ultimately, threatening democracy and a civil way of life

Adapted from https://guides.monmouth.edu/media_literacy/ConspTheories.

Table 6.2 Why Does it *Seem* Like Conspiracy Theories are More Common Now?

- Influence of media—especially the Internet—available 24/7.
- Influence of social media sites and easy communication among homemade theorists.
- The COVID pandemic—difficult to understand a worldwide plague killing nearly 100 million people.
- Free mainstream media publicity given to extreme theories and behaviors (e.g., QAnon).
- Increased political polarization in American society.
- Influence of conspiracy plots in movies and TV (see below).
- Disappearance of the Fairness Doctrine (see below).
- Increasing distrust of national political and health leaders.
- Increasing distrust of experts.
- Lack of Civics teaching in public schools and fear of teachers to discuss Civics.

9/11 conspiracists claimed that American Airlines flight 77 did not actually crash into the Pentagon. They pointed to the absence of the explosion at the moment of impact as the evidence. But the video had such a low number of frames per second that it missed it. That fact did not dissuade them, however, and they often expanded their theory into asserting that the NY tower explosions were "false flag" operations by our own government.

As conspiracy theories have seemingly become more widespread and more dangerous, it is crucial to understand why people believe them (in the hopes of possibly minimizing the damage they can do in the future) (Table 6.2).

SIGN OF THE TIMES

Figure 6.1 Copyright © Cartoon Bank. Used with permission.

THE INTERNET IS THE KEY TO TRANSMISSION

The Internet has become the key vehicle for dissemination of conspiracy theories, and it is a powerful one. Pre-Internet, it took pamphlets or newsletters or specialized books and expensive-to-make videos sold only by mail-order to let fly with a conspiracy theory. Now? Spread occurs instantaneously, like wildfire. Even many years ago, searches for "conspiracy" yielded close to thirty million results on Google (Byford, 2015). More recently, the advent of video-sharing sites like YouTube (2005) and Google Videos (2005) has accelerated the pace. Talk Radio—especially right-wing conservative Talk Radio—and Fox TV (1986) are not far behind.

Politicians and commentators have latched on to the Internet in increasing numbers because of their new-found ability to spread unfounded and sometimes totally false information that might increase their poll numbers or viewership. Trump was known as the "conspiracy candidate" during the 2016 election and put forth a variety of conspiracy theories including his Birther controversy (again, disproven with the actual Obama birth certificate but that satisfied few of Trump's supporters), and later his Big Lie assertion that the 2020 election had been "stolen" from him. The political and financial gains seem to outweigh the need for accuracy and responsibility. "In addition, in the current political moment, there are a number of nonstate actors, many operating in fringe media outlets, who traffic in conspiracy theories, usually of this same outlandish and political smear-focused variety. That politicians and other actors are spreading large numbers of these fictive narratives, apparently for personal and financial gain, is troubling and potentially corrosive to democratic governance (Jimenez, 2019)."

But sadly, deploying conspiracy theories as a political tool is not new, although seemingly far more effective and dangerous now. Consider that opposition politicians in Britain in the late 1800s wanting to gain support for conscription and defense spending reported that there was a German conspiracy to invade Britain (Jimenez, 2019). Of course, with Hitler and his lethal conspiracy theories, that actually came later.

Most people—having grown up with conspiracies occurring almost daily in their fictional media—don't realize how prominently they are featured in mainstream entertainment media:

There are many classic examples. On TV, *The X-files* and more recently *24* and Homeland:

In the movies, *Wag the Dog*, *JFK*, and *3 Days of the Condor*.

In fiction, anything by Dan Brown: *The Da Vinci Code* (2003), *Angels and Demons* (2000), *The Lost Symbol* (2009).

The basic difference between human beings and other animals is that we live in a world directed by the stories we tell. Most of what we know, or think we know, we have never personally experienced, but heard from stories. They confer the ability to socialize a culture. The ultimate shaping of human behavior comes from the stories that we hear and tell from infancy on. We're born into a culture in which these stories begin to develop our sense of self, and our sense of life, and the world, and society (Jhally, 1997).

These days, people no longer get their news—especially their political news—from the news (TV newscasts, radio, newspapers). Thanks to the Internet, social networking sites, iPads, and smartphones, they get their news from entertainment shows—that is, movies and TV. And that "news" is fictional, not real (Prior, 2005). It often contains plots that are completely relevant to social or political problems and themes, with an emphasis on trying to be as realistic as possible. Because of the skill of TV and movie producers in creating engrossing and realistic plots, viewers may be led into thinking what they are seeing is somehow real. Fiction becomes reality.

There is no question that people, especially children, *learn* important attitudes and even behaviors from the media. The pediatric, psychology, and communications literature is full of studies attesting to the influence of the media on young people at least when it comes to media violence, sex in the media, body self-imagery, obesity, depression, and suicide, and substance use (Strasburger et al., 2014). How much adults are affected is more arguable, but

Figure 6.2   Famous Conspiracy Movies.

Figure 6.2   Continued.

Figure 6.2   Continued.

Figure 6.2 Continued.

Figure 6.2 Continued.

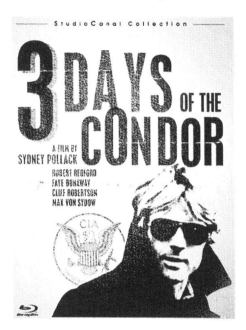

Figure 6.2   Continued.

there is a smattering of studies showing that entertainment media can, in fact, affect political beliefs and attitudes at least.

- Exposure to a film about a Communist take-over of the United States (*Amerika*) resulted in increased fears about Russia among viewers (Lenart & McGraw, 1989).
- Viewers assigned to either a positive or a negative portrayal in *Law & Order* of the criminal justice system were affected by those portrayals, especially if they identified with the characters (Mutz & Nir, 2010).
- African-Americans viewing the movie *Malcolm X* were found to become more concerned about race relations and more race conscious (Davis & Davenport, 1997).
- Other studies have shown that TV dramas can increase the importance of crime or health care in people's views, can frame political attitudes about sensitive issues like abortion, and can actually cause viewers to confuse fact and fiction. "Readers rely on fiction as a source of information, even when fiction contradicts relatively well-known facts about the world" (Marsh & Fazio, 2006, p. 1140). There are actually two other studies which specifically address conspiracy thinking:
  ○ Exposing subjects to incorrect information about Princess Diana's death changed their views of why she was killed in a car crash (Douglas & Sutton, 2008).

○ Viewers of Oliver Stone's conspiracy-based *JFK* in a theater sample bought into Stones' erroneous parts of the Kennedy assassination.

However, both studies suffered from methodological flaws (Butler et al., 1995). But in regards specifically to media and conspiracy theories, there are two very underappreciated pieces of supportive evidence: the role of cultivation theory, and one unique experiment.

THE ROLE OF CULTIVATION THEORY

People who view a lot of television (and, presumably, movies) are more likely to believe that the fictional world they're seeing is actually the real world according to cultivation theory (Gerbner et al., 1986; Morgan et al., 2009). Their beliefs tend to coincide with what they are viewing on the screen. Therefore, it makes sense that if they are seeing conspiracy after conspiracy on TV and in movies, they would be more likely to believe in real-life conspiracy theories.

As the author of *Suspicious Minds: Why We Believe Conspiracy Theories* observes (Brotherton, 2015, pp. 156–157):

> The stories we listen to can influence our beliefs and behavior. When you want to persuade someone, a story can be infinitely more effective than a mere list of bullet points . . . stories lure us in, bypassing our critical faculties. When we know someone is trying to persuade us, we are likely to scrutinize their arguments, but stories can shape our beliefs without us even realizing it. The better a story is, the more we are engrossed in it; the more engrossed we are, the more we are open to persuasion.

Is there any proof that this is the case? Sadly, not very much. There is currently no content analysis of TV or movies that totals up the number of shows with conspiracies seen per hour, nor has there been any attempt to correlate heavy media viewing with an increased susceptibility to believe in conspiracy theories. But the presence of conspiracies in TV dramas and movies is undeniable—Type "conspiracy-government" into *IMDB.com* and you get a list a mile long.

There are films that are rife with conspiracies about the government (*Enemy of the State*, my favorite), a government cover-up (*All the President's Men*, *JFK*) the CIA (any Bourne movie), Russia (*The Manchurian Candidate*), big business conglomerates (*Michael Clayton, Class Action*), an innocent man framed for murder (*The Fugitive*), an innocent man mistaken for someone else (*North by Northwest*), bent cops (*Serpico, Training Day*), the Catholic

Church (*Spotlight, The Verdict*), Nazis (*Conspiracy*), an unknown stranger (*Shadow of a Doubt*), a philandering husband or wife (*Fatal Attraction, Gone Girl, Unfaithful*), the evil organization trying to take over the world (any Bond movie)—the list goes on and on. Television series are no slouch either, with classics like *The X-Files, 24,* and more recently *Stranger Things* and *Bosch* (Wikipedia, 2022).

That said, there is a fascinating study showing the impact of conspiracies in popular media, using *Wag the Dog*—a thoroughly enjoyable movie (highly recommended), starring Robert DeNiro and Dustin Hoffman.

"WAG THE DOG" EXPERIMENT
(MULLIGAN & HABEL, 2013)

In the movie, an American president from an undisclosed political party is discovered in a sex scandal in the middle of his reelection campaign. His political consultant (played by Robert DeNiro) convinces him to hire a famous film producer (played by Dustin Hoffman) to stage a fake war with Albania in a Hollywood studio to distract the public's and the media's attention from the scandal. The film is obviously a very broad satire on political shenanigans within American democracy since the president and his consultants are seen as being able to do whatever they want, including faking a war (note the obvious relevance to recent events).

Hoffman's character hires actors (including Woody Harrelson, fake military hero) to create realistic footage that is shown on every TV channel, and the plan works! Coverage of the scandal disappears, coverage of the "war" is nonstop, and the American public rallies round the flag.

Would viewers believe that the possibility of faking a war is real—a genuine political conspiracy?

The researchers recruited 191 subjects from an introductory college political science course and randomized them into two groups, one control (ninetynine), one treatment (ninety-two). All were shown the following scenarios, but the control group was shown them and then participated in a completely different study while the treatment group was shown them after viewing the film:

Slide 1 Consider a scenario in which an American president—any president who has been elected in the past or may be elected in the future—faces a scandal that causes the president's opinion poll ratings to go down.

Slide 2 In order to increase his opinion ratings—say, during his reelection campaign, or for some other reason—the president and his assistants work with a film producer to stage a fake war.

Slide 3 The intention is not actually to go to war. Rather, the intention is to create fake video scenes of a war so that the news media and citizens will think the country is at war.

Slide 4 The video footage of the fake war is given to members of the news media, who think they are real, and play them on television as if they were real.

Slide 5 The news media and the public think the country has gone to war. They rally around the president during this time of trouble. The president's opinion poll ratings go way up.

After viewing the slides, all subjects were asked two questions and were asked to respond on a 6-point Likert scale from Extremely Unlikely to Extremely Likely:

1. "How likely is it that a U.S. president WILL stage a fake war IN THE FUTURE?"
2. "Generally speaking, how likely is it that a U.S. president HAS ACTUALLY STAGED a fake war in the past?"

The results were as expected—the treatment group was more likely to sign on to the conspiracy theory that wars could be faked for political advantage in the future or had been in the past.

Granted, this is only one study and one film, but it was well constructed, it follows directly in the mainstream findings of media research showing media's power to influence and educate, and imagine "multiplying" it by hundreds of TV show and movies. In short, fiction matters! And the cultivation effect is alive and well.

Consider the implications: if one fictional film can alter viewers' perceptions about a very significant social/political event—war—imagine what a diet of conspiracy plots in TV and movies does day after day, particularly beginning with young viewers who do not have the intellectual discriminatory powers of adults. Media researchers interested in why people believe in conspiracy theories need to look harder at fiction in all its forms (TV, movies, books) rather than just demographics and new media.

SOLUTIONS

Potential solutions do exist, although they may not be immediately apparent to frustrated people who have to deal with conspiracy theories seemingly constantly these days.

Victor C. Strasburger

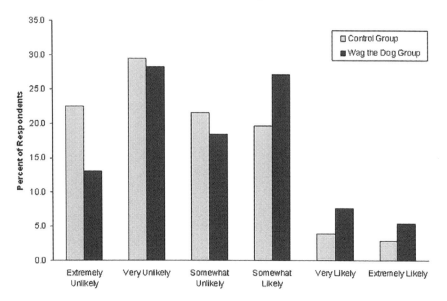

Figure 6.3   Distribution of Beliefs in a Future Fake War. "How likely is it that a U.S. president WILL stage a fake war IN THE FUTURE?" Participants randomly assigned to watch Wag the Dog (N = 92) or control group (N = 99). *Source*: ©Elsevier Publishing.

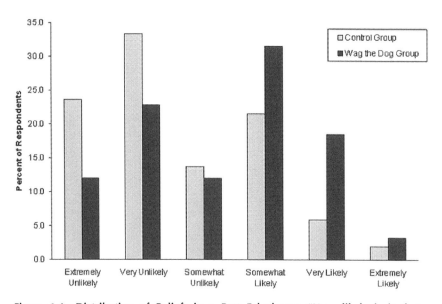

Figure 6.4   Distribution of Beliefs in a Past Faked war. "How likely is it that a U.S. president HAS ACTUALLY STAGED a fake war in the past?". *Source*: ©Elsevier Publishing.

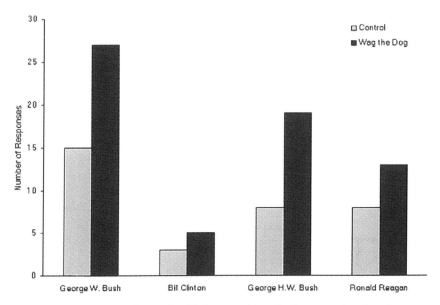

Figure 6.5   Actual Presidents Identified as Having Faked a War. The sixty-four participants who said that it is at least "Somewhat" likely that a president has faked a war (thirty-seven in Wag the Dog group and twenty-seven in the control condition) were then asked "Which (if any) of these presidents likely staged a fake war?". *Source:* ©Elsevier Publishing.

1. Tell it like it is (to quote Howard Cosell). American media need to fulfill their public service role and tell the news accurately and fairly. Don't call it conspiracy theory, call it disinformation, or outright lies—which is what the media are currently doing when they refer to the 2020 election and the Big Lie. The media were notoriously slow to call out candidate Trump in 2016 for his lies and misstatements, but they possibly have gradually warmed to their responsibility to the general public and are now seem quicker to analyze and criticize politicians of any political persuasion. But given the pervasiveness of conspiracy theories and outright lies in American politics, it may be too little too late.

The media have simply lost the public's trust, and they need to regain it. In 2003, 54 percent of Americans said that had a great deal of fair amount of trust in the media. By 2013, that number fell slightly to 44 percent. But with Trump's constant attacks on the media, just 32 percent trusted the media in 2016, and the political breakdown was eye-opening—only 14 percent of Republicans thought the media tells the truth compared with 51 percent of Democrats (Brenan, 2021).

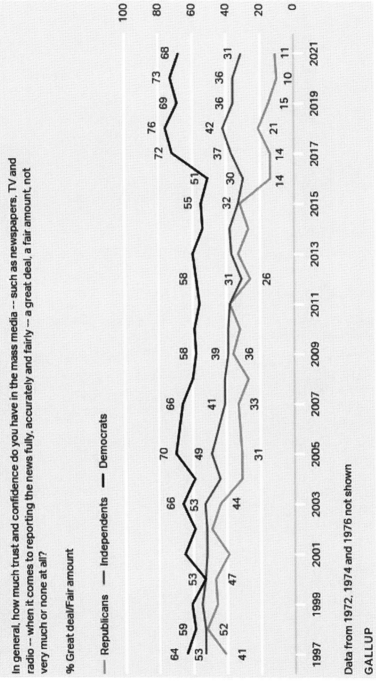

Figure 6.6 Copyright © Gallup Inc. Used with permission.

2. Try to understand conspiracists. It may be very helpful to understand the nature of conspiracy-minded people because misconceptions are common. Many authors have proposed a variety of caveats about trying to educate people about conspiracy theories (see Brotherton, 2015; Sunstein, 2014, for example):

   a. Believers are not necessarily intellectually inferior or simple-minded. They are not (necessarily) "lunatics, kooks, or paranoiacs" (Byford, 2015).

   b. Most of us have only very limited knowledge of the very complex world we live in. Therefore, it is virtually impossible to actually know all of the facts. People don't like to think that very important events are occurring randomly or by luck. Conspiracy theories fill an important void for certain people. "Conspiracy theorizing is, in a sense, built into the human condition" (Sunstein, 2014, p. 3).

   c. It is impossible to talk someone out of believing in a conspiracy theory, even using facts. Nothing can disprove the conspiracy.

   d. Lack of evidence means *the conspiracy is working*.

   e. Part and parcel of any conspiracy theory is that the ultimate truth is just out of reach for mere mortals.

   f. "One person's conspiracy theory is the next person's conspiracy fact" (Brotherton, p. 64) .

   g. People don't tend to buy into just one conspiracy theory.

There is legitimate debate about where conspiracy theorists land on the political spectrum. While it is tempting to blame conservative Republicans for promulgating the bulk of conspiracy theories—and certainly the Big Lie would seem to support that idea—experts in the field feel that the spectrum goes both ways, both Republican and Democrat.

3. Re-instate the Fairness Doctrine. One fairly easy solution would be for the Federal Communications Commission (FCC) to resurrect the Fairness Doctrine. "Arguably the most famous—and most maligned and misunderstood—media policy ever enacted in the United States, its long, strange history is generally not well known. Yet it holds important implications for growing concerns about disinformation, ownership and control of our news and information systems, the rights of audiences and the future of our democracy" (Pickard, 2021). This was a policy introduced in 1949 which required broadcasters to present both sides of controversial issues in a fair manner.

   Remember that there were only three major networks at the time, and no cable TV, so the FCC was concerned that they might present a very biased agenda to the public (sound like FOX?). Congress agreed in 1954 and in the 1970s, the FCC called the move "the single most important requirement of operation in the public interest—the *sine qua non* for grant of a renewal of license" (Fletcher, 2009). Despite the U.S. Supreme Court's total protection of the First Amendment, the Court actually upheld the Doctrine unanimously in a 1969 case, *Red Lion Broadcasting Co. v. FCC.* The Court determined that "It is the right of the viewers and listeners, not the right of the broadcasters, which is paramount" in hearing diverse information. ("Red Lion Broadcasting Co. v. FCC." *Oyez,* www.oyez.org/cases/1968/2. Accessed May 28, 2022.)

The doctrine was slowly ended during Reagan's second term in office and repealed altogether by the FCC in 1987 after a 1986 DC Circuit Court decision (with Justices Robert Bork and Antonin Scalia on the bench) weakening it substantially. Ending the Doctrine was actually one of the prime contributors to the rise of right-wing Talk Radio in the 1990s. Attempts to revive it have predictably met with furious opposition by conservatives—Rush Limbaugh called the Fairness Doctrine just "the tip of the iceberg" of an attempt by the federal government to expand its power and to "Hush Rush," Newt Gingrich called the Fairness Doctrine "Affirmative Action for liberals" and Sean Hannity called it "an assault on the First Amendment" (Fletcher, 2009).

While the Doctrine wouldn't put talk radio out of business or even force radio stations to give equal time to alternative perspectives (since radio is not regulated the same way as TV[1]), it might restore some sanity to various political assertions on TV and rein in some of the absurd pronouncements on certain networks. The Doctrine is more than a requirement for "equal time," however. It puts the burden of responsibility on broadcasters to cover important issues to the public in an intelligent fashion, allowing for differing and diverse perspectives, essentially *educating* the public.

Re-implementing the Fairness Doctrine could be a vital part of bolstering American democracy, in a time when it is threatened by unbalanced reporting and commentary: "Today, like the 1940s, we must confront dangerous concentrations of unaccountable media power and attendant disinformation about public health, elections, insurrections and other life and death issues. Although imposing dubious regulatory corrections onto run-amok commercial systems are of limited utility, new public interest obligations for our digital age could be part of the solution" (Pickard, 2021).

4. Teach children media literacy (see Frank Baker's chapter in this volume).
   Media literacy—also now called media education—has been shown in

---

[1] TV is regulated under the 1934 Federal Communications Act, which states in part that the public owns the airwaves, and they are leased back to stations to produce content in the public's best interests and to deal with controversial topics!

numerous studies to be effective in "immunizing" children against harmful media effects. (McCannon, 2014; Rosenkoetter et al., 2008; Pinkleton & Austin, 2008; Primack & Hobbs, 2009; Primack et al., 2009; Moreno et al., 2009). Unfortunately, media literacy does not begin with an "R" because it would be the fourth "R" with Reading, Writing, and "Rithmatic." Given the tsunami of information heading children's way daily and the apparent difficulty that many people have sorting out fact from fiction, teaching media literacy has now become nearly urgent (likewise Civics). A century ago, to be literate meant that someone could read and write. Now it means having the ability to decipher a bewildering away of entertainment and social media and make sense of them all. Nearly every Western country actually *mandates* some form of media education (e.g., Canada, the UK, and Australia).

5. Teach ethics in communications and journalism schools. If American democracy is going to continue intact, journalists are going to have to play an increasingly important role. In a sense, they are the "gatekeepers" to up-to-date information in American society. More care will be needed to separate actual news from commentators' opinions, and radio and TV outlets will have to occasionally curtail their obsession with ratings.

Witness, for example, "News Night" anchor Will McAvoy's apology after his cable news network failed to cover 9/11 and the events that led up to it adequately on Aaron Sorkin's HBO series. On Aaron Sorkin's HBO series (he also created and wrote *The West Wing*), world famous anchor McAvoy looks directly at the camera and confesses (Peterlin & Peters, 2019):

> Adults should hold themselves accountable for failure, so tonight I'm beginning this newscast by joining Mr. Clarke and apologizing to the American people for our failure: the failure of this program during the time I have been in charge of it to successfully inform and educate the American electorate. . . . I was an accomplice to a slow and repeated and unacknowledged and unamended train wreck of failures that have brought us to now. I'm a leader in an industry that miscalled election results, piped up terror scares, ginned up controversy and failed to report on titanic shifts in our country, from the collapse of the financial system to the truths about how strong we are, to the dangers we actually face . . . . The reason we failed isn't a mystery: We took a dive for the ratings.

6. Mandate compulsory voting. In a book chapter about conspiracies, discussing mandatory voting would seem a bit foolish, but theoretically the "good" intelligent voters would drown out the foolish mis-informed voters (Gresham's law of voting). Athenian democracy held that it was every citizen's duty to vote. Complain as much as you like about Donald

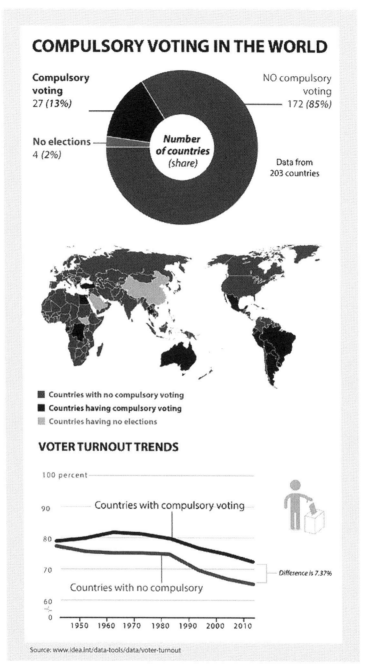

Figure 6.7 Compulsory voting is not that unusual world-wide. https://www.idea.int/
data-tools/data/voter-turnout/compulsory-voting. Copyright © International Idea. Used
with permission.

Trump's victory in 2016, of the 245.5 million Americans eligible to vote, only 137.5 million actually did so—57 percent. The turnout was better in 2020—66.7 percent voted. But that is still well below the 90+ percent of people in Belgium and Australia who vote due to mandatory voting. In fact, universal voting is used in twenty-six countries worldwide, including Argentina, Brazil, Belgium, Greece, Luxenbourg, Peru, and Uruguay (figure 6.7) (Dionne & Rapoport, 2022). In Australia, 96.3 percent of Australians are registered to vote, and nearly 92 percent of those registered actually voted. They do not necessarily have to vote for a specific candidate—they can turn in a blank ballot or write in comments.

7. Create fundamental changes in American government and politics. As *Washington Post* columnist Jennifer Rubin points out (Rubin, 2022): "Our democracy doesn't work when the will of the majority is consistently ignored (repudiated, even) by a minority out of step with the nation's views and values. This takes place primarily with four antidemocratic tools: (1) the Electoral College, which has installed Republican presidents who lack majority support; (2) thinly populated, overwhelmingly White states' disproportionate power in the Senate; (3) the filibuster, which effectively gives the minority party a veto over the majority; and (4) lifetime tenure of Supreme Court justices." Changes like these would not come easily, but again they might ensure that the minority conspiracists wind up heavily outnumbered by the more reasonable majority electorate.

Similarly, politicians need to be held to a new, higher standard—dealing in fact, not speculation or conspiracy theories, or risk losing the votes they need to win public office (Jimenez, 2019).

Ultimately, the fate of American democracy may be at stake. Yes, there are true conspiracies, but they are few and far between compared with outlandish false ones. And yes, conspiracies have existed since early civilizations, but there is little question that they are far more common—and harmful—now. Media may contribute to conspiracies in an unintentional and nearly invisible way. More research is clearly needed, especially along the lines of the *Wag the Dog* study, but the media can conceivably become part of the solution as well as now being part of the problem.

FURTHER READING

Brotherton, R. (2016). *Suspicious Minds: Why We Believe Conspiracy Theories.* London: Bloomsbury Sigma.

Byford, J. (2015). *Conspiracy Theories: A Critical Introduction.* New York: Palgrave Macmillan.

Dionne, E. J., & Rapoport, M. (2022). *100% Democracy – The Case for Universal Voting*. New York: The New Press.
Jhally, S. (1997). *The Electronic Storyteller: Television and the Cultivation of Values*. Northampton, MA: Media Education Foundation.
Olmstead, K. S. (2019). *Real Enemies: Conspiracy Theories and American Democracy, World War I to 9/11*. New York: Oxford University Press.
Sunstein, C. R. (2014). *Conspiracy Theories and Other Dangerous Ideas*. New York: Simon & Schuster.

REFERENCES

Bessi, A., Coletto, M., Davidescu, G. A., Scala, A., Caldarelli, G., & Quattrociocchi, W. (2015). Science vs conspiracy: Collective narratives in the age of misinformation. *PLoS ONE*, February 23, 2015. https://journals.plos.org/plosone/article?id=10.1371/journal.pone.0118093. Accessed June 6, 2022.
Brenan, M. (2021, October 7). Americans' trust in media dips to second lowest on record.
Brotherton, R. (2016). *Suspicious Minds: Why We Believe Conspiracy Theories*. London: Bloomsbury Sigma.
Butler, L. D., Koopman, C., & Zimbardo, P. G. (1995). The psychological impact of viewing the film JFK: Emotions, beliefs, and political behavioral intentions. *Political Psychology*, *16*, 237–257.
Byford, J. (2015). *Conspiracy Theories: A Critical Introduction*. New York: Palgrave Macmillan.
CBS News. (2022, April 18). Alex Jones' Infowars files for bankruptcy in wake of defamation suits over his assertions that the Sandy Hook massacre was a hoax. https://www.cbsnews.com/news/alex-jones-bankruptcy-filing-infowars-defamation-suits-sandy-hook/
Chigwedere, P., Seage, G. R., Gruskin, S., Lee, T. H., & Essex, M. (2008). Estimating the lost benefits of antiretroviral drug use in South Africa. *Journal of Acquired Immune Deficiency Syndrome*, *49*, 410–415.
Davis, D. W., & Davenport, C. (1997). The political and social relevancy of Malcolm X: The stability of African American political attitudes. *Journal of Politics*, *59*, 550–564.
Dionne, E. J., & Rapoport, M. (2022). *100% Democracy—The Case for Universal Voting*. New York: The New Press.
Douglas, K. M., & Sutton, R. M. (2008). The hidden impact of conspiracy theories: Perceived and actual influence of theories surrounding the death of Princess Diana. *Journal of Social Psychology*, *148*, 210–221.
Fletcher, D. (2009, February 20). A brief history of the fairness doctrine. *TIME*. http://content.time.com/time/nation/article/0,8599,1880786,00.html
Gerbner, G., Gross, L., Signorielli, N., & Morgan, M. (1986). *Television's Mean World: Violence Profile No. 14–15*. Philadelphia: University of Pennsylvania, Annenberg School of Communication.

Grant, K. R. (2019). FBI conspiracy theory redacted. https://www.scribd.com/document/420379775/FBI-Conspiracy-Theory-Redacted

Jhally, S. (1997). *The Electronic Storyteller: Television and the Cultivation of Values.* Northampton, MA: Media Education Foundation.

Jimenez, M. (2019, September 5). The truth about conspiracy theories. https://now.tufts.edu/articles/truth-about-conspiracy-theories. Accessed June 6, 2022.

Lenart, S., & McGraw, K. M. (1989). America watches Amerika: Television docudrama and political attitudes. *Journal of Politics, 51,* 697–712.

Mann, T. E., & Ornstein, N. J. (2016). Quoted in. https://www.goodreads.com/author/quotes/20870895.Thomas_E_Mann_Norman_J_Ornstein

Marsh, E. J., & Fazio, L. K. (2006). Learning errors from fiction: Difficulties in reducing reliance on fictional stories. *Memory & Cognition, 34,* 1140–1149.

McCannon, B. (2009). Media literacy/media education: Solution to big media? A review of the literature. In: Strasburger, V. C., Wilson, B. J., & Jordan, A. (Eds.), *Children, Adolescents, & the Media* (2nd ed., pp. 519–569). Thousand Oaks, CA: Sage.

Monmouth University. (2022). Media literacy & misinformation: How it spreads - Social media & conspiracy theories. https://guides.monmouth.edu/media_literacy/ConspTheories. Accessed June 6, 2022.

Moreno, M. A., VanderStoep, A., Parks, M. R., Zimmerman, F. J., Kurth, A., & Christakis, D. A. (2009). Reducing at-risk adolescents' display of risk behavior on a social networking web site. *Archives of Pediatrics & Adolescent Medicine, 163*(1), 35–41.

Morgan, M., Shanahan, J., & Signorielli, N. (2009). Growing up with television: Cultivation processes. In: Bryant, J., & Oliver, M. (Eds.), *Media Effects: Advances in Theory and Research* (3rd ed., pp. 34–49). Hillsdale, NJ: Erlbaum.

Mulligan, K., & Habel, P. (2013). The implications of fictional media for political beliefs. *American Political Research, 41,* 122–146.

Mutz, D. C., & Nir, L. (2010). Not necessarily the news: Does fictional television influence real-world policy preferences? *Mass Communication and Society, 13,* 196–217.

Olmstead, K. S. (2019). *Real Enemies: Conspiracy Theories and American Democracy, World War I to 9/11.* New York: Oxford University Press.

Peterlin, L. J., & Peters, J. (2019). Teaching journalism ethics through "The Newsroom": An enhanced learning experience. *Journalism & Mass Communication Educator, 74*(1), 44–59. https://journals.sagepub.com/doi/full/10.1177/1077695818767230. Accessed June 6, 2022.

Pickard, V. (2021, February 4). The Fairness Doctrine won't solve our problems: But it can foster needed debate. *Washington Post.* https://www.washingtonpost.com/outlook/2021/02/04/fairness-doctrine-wont-solve-our-problems-it-can-foster-needed-debate/

Pinkleton, B. E., & Austin, E. W. (2008). Effects of a peerled media literacy curriculum on adolescents' knowledge and attitudes toward sexual behavior and media portrayals of sex. *Health Communication, 23*(5), 462–472.

Primack, B. A., & Hobbs, R. (2009). Association of various components of media literacy and adolescent smoking. *American Journal of Health Behavior, 33*(2), 192–201.

Primack, B. A., Sidani, J., Carroll, M. V., & Fine, M. J. (2009). Associations between smoking and media literacy in college students. *Journal of Health Communication*, *14*(6), 541–555.

Prior, M. (2005). News vs. entertainment: How increasing media choices widens gaps in political knowledge and turnout. *American Journal of Political Science*, *49*, 577–592.

Rosenkoetter, L. I., Rosenkoetter, S. E., & Acock, A. C. (2008). Television violence: an intervention to reduce its impact on children. *Journal of Applied Developmental Psychology*, *30*(4), 381–397.

Rubin, J. (2022, June 5). Democrats should be clear: A radical GOP is holding the country back. *Washington Post*. https://www.washingtonpost.com/opinions/2022 /06/05/abortion-guns-gop-democrats-must-focus-on-gop-extremism/

Strasburger, V. C., Wilson, B. J., & Jordon A. B. (2014). *Children, Adolescents, and the Media* (3rd ed.). Thousand Oaks, CA: Sage.

Sunstein, C. R. (2014). *Conspiracy Theories and Other Dangerous Ideas*. New York: Simon & Schuster.

Wagner, B. (2021, June 6). Fact check: Hillary Clinton was not hanged at Guantanamo Bay. *USA Today*. https://www.usatoday.com/story/news/factcheck/2021/06/17/ fact-check-hillary-clinton-not-hanged-guantanamo-bay/7687922002/

Wikipedia. (2022). List of conspiracy-thriller films and television series. https://en .wikipedia.org/wiki/List_of_conspiracy-thriller_films_and_television_series

Chapter 7

How Media Literacy Could Save the World

Frank W. Baker

"News and media literacy is a critical skill impacting students' academic, personal, professional and civic lives." Shaelynn Farnsworth, director of education, The News Literacy Project[1]

"What has become abundantly clear after nearly two years of the pandemic and the current political landscape is that schools need to focus on media literacy."[2]

"Interest in media literacy and media education has moved from being somewhat marginal to being far more main-stream as we come to realize the importance of helping young people."[3]

"It is a genuine challenge to convince people to consider news they are disinclined to trust for ideological reasons even when that reporting is based on well-founded evidence. To foster that attitude toward news, we need critical media literacy education."[4]

"I think that we are seeing, indeed, a greater connectivity between misinformation and false narratives on social media and the threat landscape." Homeland Security Secretary Alejandro Mayorkas, quoted in The Hill[5]

"What is needed (to combat fake news) is more relentless, sophisticated and unyielding pressure on the superspreaders of misinformation."[6]

"Information disorder is a crisis that exacerbates all other crises. When bad information becomes as prevalent, persuasive, and persistent as good information, it creates a chain reaction of harm."[7]

AN UPDATE

So much has changed since I originally authored this chapter for this publication: fake news and disinformation, from foreign and domestic sources have exploded. The ability of people, including young people, to discern fact from fiction is a major problem for education. Social media companies are under increasing pressure to remove controversial and damaging content. Schools, already under pressure to deal with the pandemic and deliver instruction, do not appear to be ready to deal with the issue of "media illiteracy."

I agree with many of my colleagues who have concluded: the problem is NOT fake news, but rather the problem is a lack of critical thinking education.

The challenge for educators continues to be: how to find time in an already crowded curriculum to teach media literacy skills. Another challenge is how ill-prepared many educators feel in dealing with fake news and controversial issues.

But all is not lost. Many organizations have risen to the occasion recognizing the urgent need to educate consumers, including young people.

The NCTE published its Task Force on Critical Media Literacy (https://ncte.org/critical-media-literacy/) offering educators guidance on how to address and implement it in the classroom.

The News Literacy Project developed Checkology, (https://checkology.org) a free school curriculum, which is designed to engage students in critical thinking about the news as well as helping them better understand how journalists verify information. The group sponsors a News Literacy Week in January of each year. (In 2022, the NEWSY cable news network, owned by the E. W. Scripps Company, aired daily segments with experts on the need for media and news literacy. Scripps is also a funder of The News Literacy Project.)

CyberCivics (https://www.cybercivics.com/) has developed a "digital literacy" curriculum for middle grades.

The Center for Media Literacy offers a free, ninety-minute online course, "Global Online Ramp to Media Literacy" (https://www.medialit.org/course/on-ramp-media-literacy/#/) which includes texts, videos, quizzes, and infographics.

The Associated Press, Reuters, and Agence France Presse, three international news gathering operations have joined a dozen groups in producing regular fact-checking columns.

Each of the sixty-eight television stations owned by TEGNA in the United States, now broadcast weekly VERIFY segments in their news broadcasts. All of the previously aired features are streamed on YouTube: (https://www.youtube.com/channel/UCnI90RlIs3yUCDCSVLLGeUA)

The *Washington Post* publishes a weekly "How To Read This Chart" designed to help readers better understand infographics. Graphic literacy is so important today because more information is delivered in visual forms.

The New York Times Learning Network offers a similar monthly feature for educators entitled: "What's Going On In This Chart"?

The documentary "Trust Me" (https://www.trustmedocumentary.com/) which examined the problem and impact of fake news and disinformation and emphasized the need for media literacy education, was broadcast by PBS stations nationwide. A companion teacher guide was developed by The News Literacy Project.

The author, along with University of Rhode Island Professor Renee Hobbs of the Media Education Lab cohosted a dozen webinars (https://mediaeducationlab.com/events) designed to engage educators in media literacy concepts and ideas for classroom implementation.

SAVE THE WORLD?

I want to be the first to acknowledge that I did not come up with the title for this chapter. Nor do I believe that media literacy can "save the world." I do however believe, that students, properly instructed in media literacy, can better understand how media messages are created and can see through "fake news," click bait, bias, and propaganda that are so prevalent today.

To paraphrase Thomas Jefferson: for a democracy to thrive, the electorate must be informed. What happens if the people are not informed? What then?

There are many signs that young people today are media illiterate: they don't question or think critically about the news and information they receive—aimlessly and carelessly forwarding whatever they receive via their various social media platforms. (One educator told me her students don't care if the news is "fake." If that's a widespread sentiment, then in addition to their ignorance, we must deal with their apathy.)

There are incremental signs that the U.S. education system has started to take notice of the failure of the system to adequately address how young people think about media. But change comes slowly and will not happen overnight.

Ask any K–12 educator what "media literacy" means, and you're bound to get a myriad of responses, most of which would be inaccurate. I should know: I've asked that question in every one of the hundreds of teacher workshops I've conducted in the last twenty+ years. Media literacy provides a lens through which we can better see and comprehend our increasingly mediated world. But media literacy cannot work without first an understanding of what media literacy education is and second without dedicated and trained educators. As I write this, I see no evidence that most educators understand media literacy nor are they receiving adequate training. (Many confuse it with "information literacy.")

I have been tasked here with addressing some of the challenges of media literacy in instruction and some of the possible solutions to those challenges.

If you read any news story about "fake news" since the 2016 election of Donald Trump, then you no doubt also saw references to the need for media literacy instruction as one strategy schools could be implementing in order to prepare young people for the world in which they reside. That world is one in which fake news travels faster than real news; a world in which more young people admittedly cannot distinguish "native ads" from news; a world in which many of them have trouble assessing the credibility of the information they read online.

At the time, I created a special web page for educators, Fake News Remedy Recommendations, https://frankwbaker.com/mlc/fake-news-recommendations/, so that educators could have access to resources, activities, and lesson plans to begin addressing the problem in their classrooms. On this site, there are a number of infographics—posters which could be strategically positioned in every classroom and adjacent to every computer at school so that students read and implement the advice and recommendations.

Since 2016, several news literacy organizations and other groups have produced their own classroom resources. Most notable among this group is the Stanford History Education Group's "Civic Online Reasoning" curriculum resource—https://sheg.stanford.edu/civic-online-reasoning created as a result of a major study which demonstrated young people's ignorance about online content.

Stanford professor Sam Wineburg explained the problem: "Many people assume that because young people are fluent in social media they are equally perceptive about what they find there. Our work shows the opposite to be true (Brooke, 2016)."

A companion effort, MediaWise, is aimed at getting educators to engage teens in the "Civic Online Reasoning" curriculum and at the same time create a nationwide network of teen "fact checkers."

Recognizing the lack of media literacy education in U.S. schools, MediaLiteracyNow initiated an effort to get individual state legislatures to pass laws that would make media literacy more available to students. A list of the states, and the various measures that have been passed, can be found here: https://medialiteracynow.org/

It is clear: most educators in the United States have not been properly prepared to teach their students media literacy. I sought to prove that point when I was invited to speak to educators in Michigan.

In a keynote speech I delivered in 2013 at the annual conference of the Michigan Council of Teachers of English, I asked attendees how many had received any media literacy training in their colleges of education. Of the 350+ educators in attendance, not one hand was raised. When I followed up, asking how many had received any media literacy instruction since being in the classroom, only a handful raised their hands. I concluded, you can't teach what you haven't been taught.

What is media literacy? There are many definitions but the one I believe comes closest to clearly defining it emanates from the Ontario Ministry of Education:

"Media Literacy is concerned with helping students develop an informed and critical understanding of the nature of mass media, the techniques used by them and the impact of these techniques. More specifically, it is education that aims to increase students' understanding and enjoyment of how the media work, how they produce meaning, how they are organized, and how they construct reality. Media literacy also aims to provide students with the ability to create media products (Media Lit, 1989)."

Prior to the age of the Internet, media messages were delivered by radio, television, books, newspapers, magazines, advertising, and movies. Since the Internet, we now have a myriad of other media and technology in the form of web pages, blogs, social media, mobile phones, e-tablets, computers, and more.

With many of these new media technologies have come concerns about how media/tech companies gather, use and sell information about consumer's search and purchase habits. To try to address those concerns, many schools have adopted "digital literacy" and "technology literacy" curricula which include, among other things, helping students better understand bullying, privacy, transparency, copyright, and more.

ISTE, the International Society of Technology in Education, has been at the forefront of publishing and promoting "technology standards" (https://www.iste.org/standards) for both teachers and students which many states have followed and adopted.

Common Sense Media created "Digital Citizenship" curricula for every grade level and offers materials free to schools. https://www.commonsense.org/education/digital-citizenship

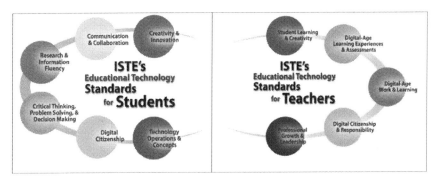

Figure 7.1   ISTE's Educational Technology for Schools.

A 2019 survey of educators found that 91 percent said that digital citizenship curricula are effective at helping students make safe, smart, and ethical decisions online (Common Sense Media, 2019).

A twenty-first century education demands that we have stronger and more vigorous instruction in visual literacy, news literacy, media literacy, and more. But alas, our education system, in 2019, is still very much print-centric.

The nation's curriculum writers have, for the most part, ignored the power and influence of the media. Almost no state acknowledges media as text.

Almost no college of education prepares new teachers for how to teach with and about the media. Almost no school library has any books for students about how media are made.

I have been teaching media literacy across the United States for more than twenty years and I have heard the same refrain from educators: "My students don't question anything—they believe everything they see, read or hear." That alone is a huge wake-up call.

At its heart, media literacy is first, and foremost about critical thinking, and applying critical thinking skills to media messages.

The Center for Media Literacy, following the lead of other media educators in Great Britain, Australia, and Canada, began in the early 1990s, to promote its Five Key Questions which correlated to the Five Core Concepts.

Read the concepts and questions here: https://www.medialit.org/reading -room/five-key-questions-form-foundation-media-inquiry

When I speak to educators, I recommend that they download and post the questions in their classrooms and refer to them every time they engage students in analyzing media messages. In order to begin to be media literate,

Five Key Questions

1. Who created this message?
2. What techniques are used to attract my attention?
3. How might different people understand this message differently from me?
4. What lifestyles, values and points of view are represented in, or omitted from, this message?
5. Why was this message sent?

Figure 7.2   Five Key Questions.

students must get accustomed to asking and researching the answers to questions like: who created this message and why; what techniques are media makers using to make a message credible; who benefits from a message being sent, and much more.

The demands on American education are huge, yet media literacy is still not on the radar screen. I should know: I have followed what every one of the fifty states says in its curriculum teaching standards. In 1999, when I coauthored an op-ed in Education Week, elements of media literacy were found in every state. Alas, those gains, were wiped out by the introduction (and adoption by forty-two states) of Common Core teaching standards.

In another Education Week commentary piece, my colleague Richard Beach and I were clear about what Common Core omitted from its English Language Arts standards: "there is no specific reference in the common standards to critical analysis and production of film, television, advertising, radio, news, music, popular culture, video games, media remixes, and so on. Nor is there explicit attention on fostering critical analysis of media messages and representations" (Beach & Baker, 2011).

Since every state decides what to teach students based on standards, the fact that Common Core Standards exclude media literacy guarantees that media literacy will neither be taught nor tested.

Yet, despite this omission, other relevant educational institutions have stepped up to the plate to recognize and promote the importance of media literacy in education.

The National Council for the Social Studies (NCSS) is promoting its College, Career, and Civic Life (C3) framework for social studies standards. The stated goals for the framework are "for states to upgrade their state social studies standards and for practitioners—local school districts, schools, teachers and curriculum writers—to strengthen their social studies programs."

A close look at the framework (above) includes "developing questions and planning inquiries," and "gathering and evaluating sources"—both of which align nicely with the goals and objectives of media literacy. https://www.socialstudies.org/c3

In the spring of 2016, NCSS published a Position Statement On Media Literacy, (https://www.socialstudies.org/publications/socialeducation/may-june2016/media-literacy). The statement provides background on media literacy as it applies to the social studies, as well as recommendations for implementing media literacy in civics, economics, history, and more. The resolution says in part:

"Through the decoding of content-rich media texts in the social studies classroom, students learn and practice the habits of asking key questions,

DIMENSION 1: DEVELOPING QUESTIONS AND PLANNING INQUIRIES	DIMENSION 2: APPLYING DISCIPLINARY TOOLS AND CONCEPTS	DIMENSION 3: EVALUATING SOURCES AND USING EVIDENCE	DIMENSION 4: COMMUNICATING CONCLUSIONS AND TAKING INFORMED ACTION
Developing Questions and Planning Inquiries	Civics	Gathering and Evaluating Sources	Communicating and Critiquing Conclusions
	Economics		
	Geography	Developing Claims and Using Evidence	Taking Informed Action
	History		

Figure 7.3   C3 Framework Organization.

applying historical analysis, identifying perspectives, assessing credibility, providing text-based evidence, drawing conclusions, and reflecting on their own process of reasoning (Sperry & Baker, 2016)."

Social studies educators are known to engage students in "primary source" documents, which among other things, includes photographs. As a result, many teachers have their students analyze and deconstruct images that accompany historical events in their textbooks and in the news.

Students of history also come in contact with media literacy when they consider how propaganda was used and how it continues to be used. Many state's standards also include studying "the rise of mass media" throughout American history.

Another area in which media literacy comes into play is "the role of the media in politics." I have written previously that the media depend on politicians, and politicians depend on the media. During elections, and especially during Presidential election years, candidate's commercials—both broadcast and streamed—become perfect fodder for study. Politicians employ advertising and PR experts to craft messages that are certain to appeal to voters. (See my website for more about this topic: https://frankwbaker.com/mlc/media-politics/)

NCSS is not the only national educational organization to recognize and recommend media literacy to teachers. In 1970, the National Council of Teachers of English (NCTE) passed a Resolution on Media Literacy (Resolution on Media Literacy, 1970).

Five years later, 1975, NCTE went even further with another Resolution on Promoting Media Literacy. It stated:

"students need to evaluate critically the messages disseminated by the mass media (Resolution on Promoting Media Literacy, 1970)."

A number of other organizations have also been strong advocates for media literacy in K–12 education.

The College Board's Standards for Student Success, in its Standards for English and Language Arts, also identifies what it means for students to be media literate (The College Board, 2006):

1. Students who are media literate communicators demonstrate knowledge and understanding of the ways people use media in their personal and public lives.
2. Media literate students know and understand the complex relationships among audiences and media content.
3. Media literate students know and understand that media content is produced within social and cultural contexts.
4. Media literate students know and understand the commercial nature of media and demonstrate the ability to use media to communicate to specific audiences.
5. Media literate students understand, interpret, analyze, and evaluate media communication.
6. Media literate students use a variety of technological and informational resources (e.g., libraries, databases, computer networks, video) to gather and synthesize information and to create and communicate knowledge.
7. Media literate students understand, interpret, analyze, and evaluate media communication.

    The K–12 Horizon Report (which identifies key trends and skills needed in education) https://www.nmc.org/publication/nmc-horizon -report-2011-k-12-edition/ concluded in 2011 that "digital media literacy continues its rise in importance as a key skill in every discipline and profession."

    The Partnership for 21st Century Learning (P21) http://www.p21.org, specifically references media literacy in its recommendations to schools: its Framework for 21st Century Learning includes media literacy as part of Information, Technology, and Media Skills.

MEDIA LITERACY'S CONNECTIONS
TO OTHER SUBJECTS

Media literacy is not confined to simply English language arts or Social Studies. In the 1999 study of state teaching standards, we found strong references to media literacy in many state's Health Education teaching standards. For example, in the National Health Standards, Standard 2 reads: "Students will analyze the influence of family, peers, culture, media, technology, and other factors on health behaviors."

This standard plays out in states in many ways, including but not limited to, studying the effect of advertising as it relates to alcohol, tobacco, and drugs; the marketing of food and drink; and body image issues.

Media literacy is also a natural fit in both our math and science classrooms. In math, students could be studying how television program ratings are generated and used. Weekly movie box office data are another great way to engage students in popular culture, math, and media literacy. The advertising industry, both print and nonprint, relies on math as it determines the cost of reaching an audience.

Science is another subject where teachers encourage student critical thinking. A perfect example is the study (reported almost daily) and how the media interprets scientific information to make it palatable for consumers. As such, "science literacy," has grown in importance in many of the nation's classrooms. In addition, the large number of science-fiction TV programs and movies begs the question: what scientific principles are portrayed accurately and which ones are not?

Media literacy is also closely aligned with the arts. Students of the visual arts, for example, are learning about "visual literacy," which involves both reading and creating images. Students of the performing arts could learn, for example, how movie music composers use certain notes and chords to convey meaning and emotion. National Media Arts standards were created in order to provide guidance to states considering adding "media arts" to its array of arts offerings. See: https://web.archive.org/web/20190126081506/http://www.mediaartseducation.org/

MEDIA ARTS PRODUCTION

For the most part, I have addressed the analysis of media messages in this chapter. Many educators also engage students in media making. With so many students owning mobile devices, the ability to take and edit photographs and videos has almost become commonplace.

There are many examples of how teachers have engaged students in media production. For example, many students create movie-style trailers based on books they have read. Other students edit productions based on assignments which involve still and moving images.

Today's digitally savvy students find media production appealing and attractive. Students have discovered, for example, how to create animations, commercials, Public Service Announcements, and more.

When students make media, they are demonstrating media literacy skills that are important and relevant.

Technology education: media literacy encourages students to ask questions of information that they read, hear, and see. Nowhere is that more important than today, when most young people get their "news" and information from their mobile devices—phones and e-tablets. So it makes sense that technology education standards throughout the United States include elements of media literacy. National Educational Technology Standards include "use technology to locate, evaluate, and collect information from a variety of sources; use technology resources for solving problems and making informed decisions" (National Educational Technology Standards for Students, 2022).

Library Media: The nation's school library media specialists are front-line educators who have helped both teachers and students understand and implement media literacy education. These libraries maintain not just books but also technology and other media. Most librarians have been trained to help students understand "information literacy" which is closely related to media literacy. National School Library Standards have been developed and promoted by the American Association of School Librarians (AASL). One of the major foundations of its standards include INQUIRE—"Build new knowledge by inquiring, thinking critically, identifying problems, and developing strategies for solving problems" (American Library Association, 2018).

FINAL THOUGHT

It is clear that media literacy instruction appears here and there in the nation's classrooms. There are a limited number of references to it in teaching standards. But having something included in standards does not guarantee it gets taught.

I have been fond of saying: what we aren't teaching students may be more important than what we are teaching them.

Every student in the United State deserves to have a strong foundation in media literacy, which I define as critical thinking about media messages.

Unfortunately they are not getting it.

Every teacher in the United States should be getting a foundation in media literacy education at the colleges and universities of education. Unfortunately, that is also not happening.

Many other groups have stepped up to provide what the American education system has ignored. That's the good news.

If you are concerned, like I am, that media literacy should get prioritized in U.S. schools, I suggest you ask your superintendent, school board member, and principal to take the necessary steps to make it happen.

NOTES

1. Napolitano, Jo, *As Misinformation Rages, Educators Focused on Improving News Literacy Turn to Outside Groups to Help Kids Parse Fact From Fantasy,* retrieved from https://www.the74million.org/article/media-news-literacy-teaching-students-misinformation-week/

2. Lowe, Pam, *Media literacy; an underrated superpower* . . .retrieved from https://www.boonvilledailynews.com/2022/01/15/media-literacy-an-underrated -superpower/

3. Reynolds, Sally, *Teachers and why they are important when it comes to Media Literacy,* retrieved from https://media-and-learning.eu/type/featured-articles/teachers -and-why-they-are-important-when-it-comes-to-media-literacy/

4. Roth, Andy Lee; Huff, Mickey, *Trustworthy News for a New Normal,* retrieved from https://www.yesmagazine.org/democracy/2022/01/04/trustworthy-news-for-a -new-normal

5. Beitsch, Rebecaa, *DHS Secretary: U.S. seeing growing connection between disinformation and domestic extremism,* retrieved from https://thehill.com/policy /national-security/588239-dhs-secretary-us-seeing-growing-connection-between -disinformation

6. Ambinder, Mark, *"Fake news" can't be fixed by more journalism, not when our democracy is broken*, retrieved from https://www.msnbc.com/opinion/fake-news-can -t-be-fixed-more-journalism-not-when-n1286563

7. Stetler, Brian, *Information disorder "creates a chain reaction of harm,"* *according to Aspen Institute report*, retrieved from https://www.cnn.com/2021/11/15 /media/information-disorder-aspen-institute-report/index.html

REFERENCES

American Library Association. (2018). AASL standards framework for learners. http:// standards.aasl.org/wp-content/uploads/2017/11/AASL-Standards-Framework-for -Learners-pamphlet.pdf

Beach, Richard, and Frank Baker . (2011, June 11). Why core standards must embrace media literacy. https://www.edweek.org/ew/articles/2011/06/22/36baker.h30.html

Donald, Brooke. (2016, November 22). Stanford researchers find students have trouble judging the credibility of information online. https://ed.stanford.edu/news /stanford-researchers-find-students-have-trouble-judging-credibility-information -online

National Educational Technology Standards for Students. https://www.kelloggllc .com/tpc/nets.pdf

Resolution on Media Literacy. (1970, November 30). http://www2.ncte.org/statement /medialiteracy/

Resolution on Promoting Media Literacy. (1975, November 30). http://www2.ncte .org/statement/promotingmedialit/

Sperry, Chris, and Frank Baker. (2016, May/June). Position statement on media lit- eracy . https://www.socialstudies.org/publications/socialeducation/may-june2016/ media-literacy

The College Board. (2006). English language arts college board standards for College Success™. http://www.asainstitute.org/conference2008/featuredsessions/colleg- eboard-english-language-arts_cbscs.pdf.

The common sense census: Inside the 21st century classroom. https://www.common-
sensemedia.org/sites/default/files/uploads/research/2019-educator-census-inside
-the-21st-century-classroom-infographic1.pdf
What is media literacy: A Canadian definition. https://www.medialit.org/reading
-room/what-media-literacy-canadian-definition

RECOMMENDED RESOURCES

Media literacy clearinghouse. http://www.frankwbaker.com
Obstacles to the development of media literacy education in the United States.
https://www.medialit.org/reading-room/obstacles-development-media-literacy-edu-
cation-united-states

Chapter 8

Does Social Media Use Contribute to ADHD?

Lloyd A. Taylor, PhD, Laura Eddy, PhD, and Erica M. Carbonell, EdS

DOES SOCIAL MEDIA CONTRIBUTE TO ADHD?

There is no denying that the rise of social media represents an important shift in how our daily lives are structured and the ways we spend our time. For better or worse, it has impacted how we interact and how we communicate. Children and adolescents who are growing up in this time period are being raised in a society in which social media is ingrained. It is important to consider potential impacts of social media and in particular, interactions with common struggles of childhood and adolescence. To that end, in this chapter we will seek to discuss some of the particular dangers of social media to children and adolescents with symptoms or diagnoses of Attention Deficit/Hyperactivity Disorder (ADHD). Describing social media is complex and the platforms are constantly changing and evolving. For simplicity, we will consider social media to be the use of digital platforms where the primary goal is interacting with others. The centrality of social media to the lives of many adolescents in the United States is an undisputed fact. However, the debate regarding potential benefits and drawbacks is ongoing.

ADHD is a highly prevalent diagnosis, impacting approximately one in twenty children. It is a neurobiological condition characterized by two primary symptom areas: inattention and hyperactivity/impulsivity (American Psychiatric Association, 2013). Symptoms of inattention can include behaviors such as trouble sustaining attention (particularly during monotonous tasks), a tendency to make careless errors, and forgetfulness. Hyperactivity/impulsivity includes behaviors such as trouble sitting still, restlessness, and a tendency to interrupt or act before thinking. Although originally considered a disorder that individuals "grew out of," it is now clear that it persists into adulthood for the majority of cases (Barkley et al., 2008).

Our understanding of the mechanisms causing ADHD is far from complete, but most researchers agree the core deficits in ADHD are deficits of inhibition. This manifests as trouble with sustaining attention and inhibiting behavior. As a result, individuals with ADHD struggle with the ability to regulate and organize goal-directed behaviors. This is reflected in the concerns reported by parents and teachers of children and adolescents with ADHD, who commonly express concerns about self-control, and describe these children and adolescents as easily distracted, particularly when working on boring, monotonous tasks such as homework or chores.

These core characteristics of ADHD may be particularly difficult to manage at this moment in time, due to advances in technology. The proliferation of smartphones and tablets has led to ongoing and widespread access to social media at all hours of the day. Resisting distraction has become infinitely more challenging for all of us. For those who already struggle to maintain focus and attention, this ongoing challenge may be particularly impactful.

The research that has been conducted on this topic is limited, but supports this notion. For instance, adolescents with ADHD reported an average of five hours of digital media use nightly (Becker & Lienesch, 2018). Children with ADHD have more time in front of a screen than their peers (Lo et al., 2015). When given access to more screens, youth with ADHD are likely to increase use. For example, when children with a diagnosis of ADHD have access to a screen in their bedroom, their average daily screen time was twenty-five minutes higher compared to those without access (95 percent) (Lo et al., 2015). Of course, high levels of daily access to devices equates to a high level of access to social media. Further compounding the problem, social media by its very nature is designed to keep users engaged. In combination with the symptoms of ADHD, this creates a perfect storm for challenges.

As noted above, technological advances have increased access to digital platforms and social media. Many people find themselves increasingly distracted by this access. As a result, some people may question whether this increased access *causes* ADHD in some way. The answer to this question is a resounding no—there is a large body of research literature that firmly establishes ADHD as a condition with a neurobiological basis that is heritable and appears early in development. It is not caused by screen use or social media. That being said, it is certainly possible that ADHD symptoms might *interact* with increased access to digital platforms and social media. In other words, the presence of ADHD symptoms may increase vulnerability to engaging in high levels of social media use; this use may in turn worsen ADHD symptoms or lead to associated difficulties. This is partially supported by research linking ADHD to "problematic" social media use.

Problematic social media use refers to use of social media that appears compulsive or addictive, marked by difficulties stopping, or problems completing responsibilities, as a result of use (Merelle et al., 2017). A large study of adolescents demonstrated associations between symptoms of ADHD and "problematic" levels of social media (Merelle et al., 2017). This suggests that higher levels of ADHD symptoms were linked to a greater likelihood of engaging in this type of use. These findings were consistent with earlier research that found symptoms of ADHD to be significantly associated with problematic social media use in adults, indicating that this association is not limited to adolescents (Andreassen et al., 2016). Further highlighting the particular risk associated with ADHD, impulsivity (a key symptom of ADHD) is positively associated with risk for problematic levels of use across multiple types of social media platforms, including Facebook, Whatsapp, and Instagram (Sindermann et al., 2020). In sum, there is mounting evidence that ADHD may serve as a particular risk factor for problematic social media use.

This is a cause for concern, as potential difficulties associated with problematic social media use are numerous. This pattern of behavior may impact multiple areas of functioning such as general health habits, academics, and social relationships. For example, there is evidence that the amount of time spent on social media is negatively correlated with academic performance (Al-Menayes, 2015). Further, engaging in more than four hours of social media use per day increases the odds of experiencing high levels of mental health difficulties—particularly symptoms of depression or anxiety (Riehm et al., 2019). Below, we discuss the potential impacts of problematic social media use on social interactions and important health behaviors (sleep and exercise).

One area of child and adolescent life in which social media may be particularly likely to have an impact is social relationships. The difficulties in social relationships and interactions experienced by individuals with ADHD are well-documented (Mikami, 2010). Some core symptoms of the disorder, such as trouble sitting still, a tendency to impulsively interrupt others, and difficulties with maintaining focus (e.g., during conversations) can lead to problems in interactions with others. For instance, children and adolescents with ADHD may be distracted when interacting with peers, or they may distract others with restless behaviors. They may speak without considering the impact of their words (impulsivity) and as a result, it may be harder for them to form and maintain friendships.

Given these struggles, it is not surprising that individuals with ADHD may also display difficulties interacting in the realm of social media. It is important to acknowledge, however, that the nature of social media platforms presents new challenges. Comments, images, and videos posted to these platforms can be stored and retained. Thus, impulsive comments or posts have the potential to not only cause immediate damage but to result in broader, more severe, and more lasting negative effects.

For example, an adolescent with ADHD may impulsively make an offensive comment online. This comment may result in conflict not only with the adolescent's peers but also could be shared with parents and school officials as well, leading to additional conflict and perhaps disciplinary action. Further, there now exists a digital record of this comment, and thus it could emerge again months or years later. Certainly, adolescents could make impulsive or insensitive comments prior to the advent of social media platforms, but the lasting nature of digital media is a new factor that can increase the potential damage of such comments.

Problematic levels of social media use may also pose a threat to important daily health behaviors, such as sleep and exercise. The greater the amount of time spent engaging in social media use, the less time is available for other activities. Consider other activities that the young person might be involved with if they were not engaged in staring at a screen or a device. There is a real disruption in daily living that occurs when social media becomes the "go to" activity for children and adolescents.

This is particularly relevant, since establishment of consistent routines helps children and adolescents diagnosed with ADHD to cope with symptoms. Consistent, healthy, patterns in wellness behaviors (e.g., sleep, nutrition, and exercise) are important for anyone, but it is particularly important in the presence of ADHD symptoms. For example, for a child with who already struggles to maintain their focus in school, fatigue due to poor sleep habits will make this problem much worse.

Sleep is an area of particular concern, since children with a diagnosis of ADHD often experience sleep difficulties. It is estimated that at least 73 percent of children and adolescents diagnosed with ADHD experience sleep problems (Sung et al., 2008). Poor sleep is linked to depression, cardiovascular disease, obesity, inattention, and concentration difficulties. A study conducted by the National Institute of Health suggests that poor sleep can cut learning by as much as 40 percent.

For a child with ADHD who may already be struggling in school, this is a serious problem. Now, there is increasing evidence that elevated use of technology and screens (often due to engaging in social media) impacts the ability to fall asleep and stay asleep among children with and without an ADHD diagnosis. Moreover, among adolescents diagnosed with ADHD more media use is associated with less sleep, more sleep problems, and increased symptoms of depression and anxiety (Becker & Lienesch, 2018). Thus, disruption to sleep is a risk associated with elevated, problematic social media use that families, health-care professionals, and educators should be aware of.

Exercise is also impacted by excessive use and involvement with social media. Time spent on social media takes away from exercise and outdoor activities. This is problematic for all youth, but particularly problematic for those diagnosed with ADHD. As with sleep, exercise is an important health behavior for anyone. The evidence for benefits of exercise is strong—exercise conveys clear health benefits for children and adolescents (e.g., decreased risk for obesity) as well as promoting psychological health (e.g., better self-esteem) (Smith et al., 2014). Additionally, this may be important for children and adolescents with ADHD, who are prone to feelings of restlessness and overactive behaviors. Exercise may help reduce feelings of restlessness and hyperactivity (Bustamante, 2016) and can therefore be an important part of a daily routine for children and adolescents with ADHD.

Advances in our understanding of the importance of exercise on learning and memory also highlight the significant impact of prolonged engagement on social media platforms. Neuroscientists have described the importance of brain-derived neurotrophic factors (BDNF) on learning and memory (Doyle & Zakrajsek, 2013). A brain with depleted BDNF essentially has difficulties learning and retaining information. Exercise is a key factor to increasing BDNF in the brain, and as such, may be important in promoting academic success. Problematic social media use can lead to a reduction in time for exercise and as a result may interfere with these important benefits.

The risks of problematic social media use discussed above are notable, yet it is also important to acknowledge and consider potential benefits of social media for youth diagnosed with ADHD. After all, social media is here to stay. Denying all access to social media seems unrealistic, unwarranted, and unnecessary. Social media platforms in and of themselves are not inherently problematic. For instance, one potential area of benefit would be facilitation of friendships. Students diagnosed with ADHD are less likely to have long-term friendships and are more likely to be low-accepted in terms of peer selection and popularity (Mikami, 2010). The widespread adoption of social media has expanded opportunities and increased the likelihood that children with ADHD can find individuals that share similar interests (Clarke, 2009). Friendships can be supported and maintained through social networking in a way that bolsters existing relationships and social ties, while simultaneously allowing for identity exploration. Social media can also provide a platform for those with ADHD to connect, share experiences and challenges, and exchange information and coping techniques.

Ultimately, it is clear social media will continue to play a significant role in all of our lives. Hence, an important question to consider is what we can do as parents, health-care professionals, and educators to help support children and adolescents with ADHD. Clearly, there is a need for knowledge and awareness of potential ramifications of social media for youth diagnosed with ADHD. As discussed above, this group is particularly vulnerable to problematic social media use, and vulnerable to disruptions in daily health behaviors. Finally, key symptoms of ADHD such as impulsivity can create particular risks in the domain of social media. Parents, health-care professionals, and educators should be informed and aware of these vulnerabilities and risks.

Further, it may be important to take intentional steps to mitigate these risks. There is evidence that restrictions and limits imposed on children and adolescents have an impact—for instance, school-aged children who are required to turn their devices off at night have been found to get an average of forty-two more minutes of sleep per night compared to their peers. Thus, there is good reason to hope that such actions can make a difference. Other potential strategies might include monitoring activity on social media platforms, placing time limits on daily social media use, requiring daily aerobic exercise, and promotion and enforcement of healthy sleep habits.

Finally, there exists a real opportunity to facilitate development of self-regulation and help youth with ADHD grow and develop insight. Specifically, we can view social media use as something that should not be avoided entirely, but rather an area in which children and adolescents need guidance and monitoring from adults to learn how to appropriately use these platforms. Engaging in open and honest conversations about the consequences of problematic social media use may be an important step, when age-appropriate. Further, adults can model appropriately limited use of social media ourselves. We can make a point of setting aside devices at the dinner table, turning these devices off at a set time each night, and taking regular time away from social media platforms.

We can also make use of clearly defined "contracts" to set clear expectations and limits for social media use. For instance, an adolescent might work with her parents to agree upon a limit of one hour for social media use on school nights after dinner. If this limit is observed each night of the week, the adolescent could earn a desired reward or privilege, such as spending time with friends on weekends. This is particularly helpful and age-appropriate for adolescents, who can be involved in negotiating the terms of the "contract," which allows them to express their opinions and perspectives. For a more detailed discussion and excellent resource on the use of contracts in treatment for families of adolescents with ADHD, see the book *Parent-teen therapy for executive function deficits and ADHD: Building skills and motivation,* by Margaret Sibley.

In sum, social media certainly presents a new area for children and adolescents to navigate. There are important risks that should be considered, as well as benefits. Parents, health-care professionals, and educators can serve as key models and sources of support as these children grow in this changing world.

REFERENCES

Al-Menayes, Jamal J. "Social media use, engagement and addiction as predictors of academic performance." *International Journal of Psychological Studies* 7, no. 4 (2015): 86–94.

American Psychiatric Association. 2013. *Diagnostic and Statistical Manual of Mental Disorders: DSM-5.* Arlington, VA: American Psychiatric Association.

Andreassen, Cecilie Schou, Joël Billieux, Mark D. Griffiths, Daria J. Kuss, Zsolt Demetrovics, Elvis Mazzoni, and Ståle Pallesen. "The relationship between addictive use of social media and video games and symptoms of psychiatric disorders: A large-scale cross-sectional study." *Psychology of Addictive Behaviors* 30, no. 2 (2016): 252–262.

Barkley, R. A., Murphy, K. R., and Fischer, M. (2008). *ADHD in Adults: What the Science Says.* New York: Guilford.

Becker, Stephen P., and Jessica A. Lienesch. "Nighttime media use in adolescents with ADHD: Links to sleep problems and internalizing symptoms." *Sleep Medicine* 51 (2018): 171–178.

Bourchtein, Elizaveta, Julie S. Owens, Anne E. Dawson, Steven W. Evans, Joshua M. Langberg, Kate Flory, and Elizabeth P. Lorch. "Is the positive bias an ADHD phenomenon? Reexamining the positive bias and its correlates in a heterogeneous sample of children." *Journal of Abnormal Child Psychology* 46, no. 7 (2017): 1395–1408.

Bustamante, Eduardo E., Catherine L. Davis, Stacy L. Frazier, Dana Rusch, Louis F. Fogg, Marc S. Atkins, and David X. Marquez. "Randomized controlled trial of exercise for ADHD and disruptive behavior disorders." *Medicine and Science in Sports and Exercise* 48, no. 7 (2016): 1397.

Cerrillo Urbina, Alberto José, Antonio García Hermoso, Mairena Sánchez López, María Jesús Pardo Guijarro, J. L. Santos Gómez, and Vicente Martínez Vizcaíno. "The effects of physical exercise in children with attention deficit hyperactivity disorder: A systematic review and meta-analysis of randomized control trials." *Child: Care, Health and Development* 41, no. 6 (2015): 779–788.

Clarke, Barbie H. "Early adolescents' use of social networking sites to maintain friendship and explore identity: Implications for policy." *Policy & Internet* 1, no. 1 (2009): 55–89.

Doyle, Terry, and Todd Zakrajsek. *The New Science of Learning: How to Learn in Harmony with Your Brain* (1st ed.). Sterling, VA: Stylus, 2013.

Lo, Charmaine B., Molly E. Waring, Sherry L. Pagoto, and Stephenie C. Lemon. "A television in the bedroom is associated with higher weekday screen time among youth with attention deficit hyperactivity disorder (ADD/ADHD)." *Preventive Medicine Reports* 2 (2015): 1–3.

Mérelle, Saskia Y. M., Annet M. Kleiboer, Miriam Schotanus, Theresia L. M. Cluitmans, Cornelia M. Waardenburg, Danielle Kramer, Dike Van de Mheen, and Tony van Rooij. "Which health-related problems are associated with problematic video-gaming or social media use in adolescents? A large-scale cross-sectional public health study." *Clinical Neuropsychiatry* 14, no. 1 (2017): 11–19.

Mikami, Amori Yee. "The importance of friendship for youth with attention-deficit/ hyperactivity disorder." *Clinical Child and Family Psychology Review* 13, no. 2 (2010): 181–198.

Riehm, Kira E., Kenneth A. Feder, Kayla N. Tormohlen, Rosa M. Crum, Andrea S. Young, Kerry M. Green, Lauren R. Pacek, Lareina N. La Flair, and Ramin Mojtabai. "Associations between time spent using social media and internalizing and externalizing problems among US youth." *JAMA Psychiatry* 76, no. 12 (2019): 1266.

Sibley, Margaret H. *Parent-Teen Therapy for Executive Function Deficits and ADHD: Building Skills and Motivation.* New York: Guilford Publications, 2016.

Sindermann, Cornelia, Jon D. Elhai, and Christian Montag. "Predicting tendencies towards the disordered use of Facebook's social media platforms: On the role of personality, impulsivity, and social anxiety." *Psychiatry Research* 285 (2020): 112793.

Smith, Jordan J., Narelle Eather, Philip J. Morgan, Ronald C. Plotnikoff, Avery D. Faigenbaum, and David R. Lubans. "The health benefits of muscular fitness for children and adolescents: A systematic review and meta-analysis." *Sports Medicine* 44, no. 9 (2014): 1209–1223.

Sung, Valerie, Harriet Hiscock, Emma Sciberras, and Daryl Efron. "Sleep problems in children with attention-deficit/hyperactivity disorder." *Archives of Pediatrics & Adolescent Medicine* 162, no. 4 (2008): 336.

Taylor, Lloyd A., Conway Saylor, Kimberly Twyman, and Michelle Macias. "Adding insult to injury: bullying experiences of youth with attention deficit hyperactivity disorder." *Children's Health Care* 39, no. 1 (2010): 59–72.

Thoma, Vanessa K., Yoanna Schulz-Zhecheva, Christoph Oser, Christian Fleischhaker, Monica Biscaldi, and Christoph Klein. "Media use, sleep quality, and ADHD symptoms in a community sample and a sample of ADHD patients aged 8 to 18 years." *Journal of Attention Disorders* 24, no. 4 (2020): 576–589.

About the Contributors

Frank W. Baker is an internationally recognized media literacy educator. For more than twenty years, he has conducted workshops with teachers. He maintains the popular Media Literacy Clearinghouse website. His most recent books include *Close Reading the Media* and *Media Literacy in the K-12 Classroom*, 2nd edition. In September 2022, *We Survived the Holocaust*—a graphic novel—was published.

Graceson L. Clements is the lab coordinator in the Espelage Research Addressing Violence in Education (RAVE) at the University of North Carolina at Chapel Hill School of Education.

Dorothy L. Espelage, PhD, is a William C. Friday Distinguished Professor of Education at the University of North Carolina at Chapel Hill and author of over 300 publications on bullying, youth violence, and social-emotional learning interventions in K-12 settings.

Dr. Susan Eva Porter spent her career working as a clinician and administrator in schools, most recently as head of school at Orinda Academy, an independent high school in the SF Bay Area that supports students with learning differences. She's also the author of two books, *Relating to Adolescents: Educators in a Teenage World* (2009) and *Bully Nation: Why America's Approach to Childhood Aggression Is Bad for Everyone* (2013), and many articles on adolescent development, parenting, and working with teens. Sue is currently in private practice, where she focuses on adolescent psychotherapy and parent coaching. She can be reached at doctor-susaneva-porter.com.

Luz E. Robinson is a doctoral candidate in school psychology at the University of North Carolina at Chapel Hill. Her research interests include culturally responsive assessments and interventions, social and emotional skills, school-based violence prevention, and mental health promotion among Latinx and other marginalized youth.

Ellison Starnes is a JD candidate at the University of Akron School of Law.

Cagil Torgal is a PhD candidate in the Department of Psychology at the University of Florida and author of several publications on cyberbullying.

Alberto Valido is a graduate student in applied developmental science and special education at the Peabody School of Education, University of North Carolina at Chapel Hill. Valido's research interests include intersectionality with a mental health prevention focus and randomized clinical trials, specifically among adolescents who experience discrimination or are victimized at school due to their sexual, racial, or gender identities.

Harry Zimmerman is an attorney with a trial or appellate practices, since 1981, appearing in courts of the United States, California, and New Mexico. His career has been devoted to the principles of the United States Constitution, whether as prosecutor or defense counsel. The focus of his defense practice has been representing indigent defendants in both state and federal courts.

Lloyd "Chip" Taylor, PhD is professor and head of the Department of Psychology at The Citadel, The Military College of SC. His research and clinical expertise are in the areas of pediatric psychology and ADHD.

Laura Eddy, PhD, is an assistant professor of psychology at The Citadel, The Military College of SC. Her research interests include ADHD in emerging adults.

Erica Carbonell, Ed.S., is a school psychologist working in the public school system in South Carolina.

ABOUT THE EDITORS

Dr. Victor Strasburger is currently founding chief of the Division of Adolescent Medicine and distinguished professor of pediatrics emeritus at the University of New Mexico School of Medicine in Albuquerque, New Mexico. He is a published novelist, having studied fiction writing at Yale with Robert Penn Warren. Dr. Strasburger has authored more than 200 articles and papers and 15 books on the subjects of adolescent medicine, and on the effects of television on children and adolescents. His most recent book prior to this one and volumes 1 and 2 of the Masters of Media series is *The Death of Childhood: Reinventing the Joy of Growing Up* (2019). His biography is available on Wikipedia and website is www.drvictorstrasburger.com

Marjorie Hogan, MD, is a professor of pediatrics at the University of Minnesota and a recently retired pediatrician in Minneapolis. In addition to decades of experience in general pediatrics and adolescent medicine, she educated and wrote about the impact of media in child and teen health.